D1326383

Colin
Edwards

Dedication

For Gracie and Holly!

Acknowledgements

A massive thanks to the following four gentlemen, without whom the book could not have been done in such a short timescale!
Colin Edwards (the first)
Tom Halverson
Jim Press (check out the official website at www.ceracing.com or www.colinedwardsii.com)
Colin Edwards (the second)
Thanks for all your help guys

Also a big thanks to the following…
Alyssia Edwards, Gordon Ritchie, Stuart Barker, Niall Mackenzie, Chris Moss, Kevin Schwantz, Paul Carruthers, Davide Brivio, Troy Bayliss, Colin MacKellar, Kent Kunitsugu, Chris Herring

And…
Steve Moore, Paul Carpenter and Scott Bentley at *Two Wheels Only* magazine

And finally, thanks to…
Gold & Goose, Kel Edge and Graeme Brown for their patience and pictures

© Bertie Simmonds 2003

All rights reserved. No part of this publication may be reproduced, stored in a retrieval system or transmitted, in any form or by any means, electronic, mechanical, photocopying, recording or otherwise, without prior permission in writing from the publisher.

First published in 2003

A catalogue record for this book is available from the British Library

ISBN 1 84425 011 3

Library of Congress catalog card no. 2003104826

Published by Haynes Publishing, Sparkford, Yeovil, Somerset BA22 7JJ, UK

Tel: 01963 442030 Fax: 01963 440001
Int. tel: +44 1963 442030 Int. fax: +44 1963 440001
E-mail: sales@haynes.co.uk
Website: www.haynes.co.uk

Haynes North America, Inc.,
861 Lawrence Drive, Newbury Park,
California 91320, USA

Printed and bound in England by
J. H. Haynes & Co. Ltd, Sparkford

Bibliography

World Superbikes – The First 15 years, Julian Ryder, Haynes Publishing: ISBN 1 85960 897 3
You Don't Know The Half Of It – Aaron Slight Autobiography, Phantom House Books Ltd: ISBN 0 473 07908 9
Foggy – The Explosive Autobiography, Collins Willow: ISBN 0 00 218961 5
Motocourse – years 1993-2002, Hazleton Publishing

Opposite:
Powering towards the 2002 World Superbike Championship on the Honda SP-2.
(Getty Images)

Colin
Edwards
The Texas Tornado

Bertie Simmonds

Contents

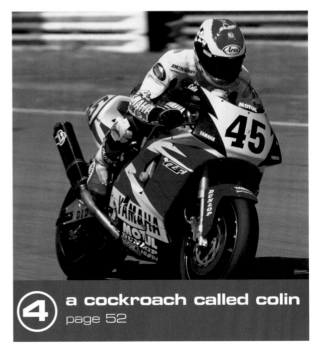

by Troy Bayliss
foreword
2001 World Superbike Champion

You don't become best mates with the people you race against, but it's fair to say Colin and I have a good relationship away from the races.

I came into the World Superbike championship in 2000 and he'd been around for a while. I knew his style: precise and smooth. I respected him.

We're similar in a few ways: like many racers we both try as hard as we can, we both want to win races and we both want to beat each other.

We all have problems in racing. He's had his fair share like the rest of us, but Colin's strong in mind. He has always believed that a true champion never gives up and if you're not winning you're not happy. He certainly never gave up in 2002.

A lot of people talk about the 2002 World Superbike season. I dominated the start, which was a bit of a surprise to be honest. But pretty soon he was clawing those points back. That didn't surprise me too much; at the start of the year I always knew it was going to be between me and him for the title.

That said, even in 2002 I didn't go to sleep thinking I had to beat Colin and I doubt he did the same, there wasn't that edge to it. He lost his title to me in 2001 and then he got it back from me in 2002 – simple as that.

I wasn't that bothered to lose the title to Colin. It was a great year's racing and a fantastic weekend at Imola. I felt I was riding better than ever, but I still lost! Sure, it would have been nice to win, but I didn't lose any sleep over it. For Colin it was a superb way to end the year.

We've had some great races together and although it looked like we were the biggest rivals out there, we could still have a beer together. He's a real easy guy to talk to, which is good, and there's no bullshit with Colin Edwards!

For the present, it's nice that we're both out there in MotoGP – Colin with Aprilia and me with Ducati.

One final thing I'd like to say is this, which is a sort of back-handed compliment. If I wasn't racing against him, I'd back him, so I'm pleased to be writing the foreword to this book.

Troy Bayliss
Monaco, May 2003

Colin and Troy at their first MotoGP race at Suzuka, Japan, April 2003. (Jim Press)

introduction

Colin Edwards II made one hell of an impact in road racing when he started out back in 1991. Winning every novice race he entered, he turned pro soon after and things got harder – just as they should do. Despite this, he won the AMA 250cc GP class first time out in 1992, racing against no less a rider than Kenny Roberts Junior. A move to AMA Superbikes on the Vance & Hines Yamaha saw tough times in the early 1990s fighting against the dominant Ducatis. There followed even tougher times in World Superbike, with a less than spectacular couple of seasons on an ageing factory Yamaha. But, Colin dug deep, did the best he could and gave it 110 per cent.

Armed with a sea of natural talent, a quick, analytical mind and a dedication to his task, Colin has risen to the top of the World Superbike pack, while many who joined the series at the same time have shone briefly and fizzled out.

His riding style, developed on 250s but with a solid background in dirt competition as a kid, is deceptively fast. He rarely looks out of shape, instead it's an almost clinically clean line, with the bike balanced on the very last atom of the razor's edge between ultimate speed and crashing. He's worked his way up to the top in World Superbikes, winning the 2000 title in the Honda VTR1000 SP-1's debut year, coming second in 2001 and then winning the 2002 title after a cliff-hanger finale. Despite being 58 points adrift at mid-season, Colin knew he could still win it when everyone else thought it was a lost cause. Such was his confidence in his ability, his machine and his team.

Now he faces his toughest challenge yet – taking the Aprilia RS3 Cube into the MotoGP class against the likes of Valentino Rossi, Max Biaggi and Kenny Roberts.

And now for the most impressive bit.

Colin Edwards, despite two world titles, Suzuka 8-Hour victories and countless race wins, is just a normal dude. Of half Aussie parentage, but undeniably Texan, he is the same guy now that he was back in 1990, when, as a skinny kid, he first threw a leg over a road-race bike. Approachable, witty, and quick with a quote for the press, he's the real-deal.

To echo Troy Bayliss's comments, in a paddock full of it, there's just no bullshit with Colin Edwards.

Bertie Simmonds
Brigstock, England, June 2003

The author becomes a 'big dipper' and foolishly accepts Colin's offer of chewing tobacco. (John Noble)

Champion again...
(Gold & Goose)

silly
season
part one

In a perfect world, the home event of your chosen sport wouldn't be like this. Colin Edwards is sitting on his Honda SP-2 at the start of the second race of the day in front of his home fans at Laguna Seca, not far inland from the Californian coast. It's Sunday, 14 July 2002. The sun is shining, Edwards is resplendent in stars and stripes leathers, and his team are all wearing ten-gallon hats straight out of Texas. The fans even know Colin's their best chance for a home win, over the likes of AMA regulars Nicky Hayden and Eric Bostrom. Laguna may be many miles from Texas, but Edwards is at home. He's been talking big, demanding nothing less than a double in front of his home fans. It doesn't get any more American than this.

It all sounds perfect, but for one thing – championship leader Troy Bayliss has started the season with a winning streak of six wins from six starts. He's had the sort of luck that makes you think his name is already on the trophy. The Australian's Ducati 998F02 positively larrups out of corners in a way that Edwards and his Honda have struggled to match, and now the defending champion has won race one in front of the American fans.

Edwards's third in race one means his dream of a home round double victory has disappeared. Now, with a 58-point deficit to make up in the remaining nine races and a seemingly invincible – and downright lucky – rider like Bayliss ahead, this mountain just seems way too big to climb.

'That afternoon was one of the biggest of my career,' says Edwards. 'I'd set pole position on the Saturday. We

Barrelling through Laguna's notorious Corkscrew with champ Troy Bayliss in tow. Like being between a rock and a hard place, especially when you're 58 points down. (Gold & Goose)

First round, Valencia, Spain. Bayliss takes two wins while Colin takes fourth and third. He, Honda and the crew had some work to do. (Gold & Goose)

had the stars and stripes livery for my home round and everything was in place for two wins. I had the edge in the first race but ran wide with about four laps to go and Troy and Ruben Xaus came by. To finish third was soul destroying. I actually felt like going home.'

But finishing in anything other than the top spot on the rostrum had been Colin's stock-in-trade up until that point. 'I'm bustin' my ass for second place,' he'd drawl for the benefit of the listening TV audience and waiting journalists during the first half of the season. And he was right.

Any other year Edwards would have been leading the World Superbike (WSB) championship by a healthy margin. But the domination shown by Bayliss – which was more total than earlier WSB gods Doug Polen and Carl Fogarty mustered during their reigns – meant that Edwards was left to pick up seconds and thirds, not the wins he needed so badly.

Bayliss and Edwards were in a class of two. Other riders had the same equipment as Troy. But while Xaus continued to push the front in his 'crash or score' start to the season and Ben Bostrom found that the Dunlops didn't always let him do what he wanted with the bike,

Bayliss had been getting on with being downright devastating. Britain's Neil Hodgson looked like being the best of the rest on a one-year-old Ducati that didn't benefit from the dominant and consistent Michelin tyres.

It was clear that Edwards was the only rider capable of catching Bayliss. He'd been strangely benefiting from a year alone, with no team-mates to help gang up on the Aussie. Chances are they wouldn't have helped anyway. Colin had been the dominant rider in the Castrol Honda set-up since 1999, beating team-mates of the calibre of Aaron Slight and 500cc GP winner Tadayuki Okada.

It's worth looking at how invincible Bayliss seemed by the end of the first two-thirds of the season. The brilliance of both men and Edwards's bottomless pit of belief is all too clear.

Round 1 Valencia

A nice way to start the season if you're the defending champion – two race wins for Bayliss and a couple of scares. He saw a bit too much red-mist in race one, over-cooking the final corner with a few laps to go, but held on to win. He even survived a sighting-lap scare on his

Crouching tiger: Colin keeps his eye on the opposition at Phillip Island... (Graeme Brown)

...And two second places was the reward. (Graeme Brown)

No 1 bike and had to take out his No 2 machine to win by more than a second. Edwards was fourth in race one – his worst result of the season – and third in race two.

Bayliss	50 points	2 Wins
Edwards	29 points	0 Wins

Round 2 Phillip Island

Taking Superpole gave Edwards heart but neither this, nor leading many of the laps in both races, made a difference. Bayliss took two more wins; Edwards took second. His Michelins seemed to lose performance compared with the Australian's. But at least Edwards was now second in the championship.

Bayliss	100 points	4 Wins
Edwards	69 points	0 Wins

Round 3 Kyalami

Another dominant double for Bayliss following another Edwards Superpole. The Texan came second in race one, but was beaten to the runner-up spot by Xaus in race two.

Bayliss	150 points	6 Wins
Edwards	105 points	0 Wins

Colin's Superpole at Kyalami, South Africa, wasn't converted into two wins. Bayliss's roll continued. (Graeme Brown)

On his way to a win at Sugo, Japan, with Haga and Tamada in pursuit. (Graeme Brown)

On your marks... Colin at Monza for round six. Comfortable leathers are a must at 180mph. (Graeme Brown)

Round 4 Sugo

Japan is a place where home stars shine, but Edwards took his first win of the year and became the first westerner to win at the Japanese round since Carl Fogarty in 1995. The home stars came back in race two with Makoto Tamada taking his SP-2 to top spot. Bayliss was happy with fifth and fourth places.

Bayliss	174 points	6 Wins
Edwards	150 points	1 Win

Round 5 Monza

Classic slip-streaming action at Monza and confusion about overshooting one of the chicanes meant that Neil Hodgson sat back to let Bayliss win, with Edwards behind him in third. Bayliss went on to win race two, this time with Edwards in second.

Bayliss	224 points	8 Wins
Edwards	186 points	1 Win

Round 6 Silverstone

Controversy raged. Bayliss dumped his bike twice but the engine carried on running, despite the supposed inclusion of a mercury-activated tilt switch. No matter, Edwards was the rain man of the moment and took race one. In race two Edwards crashed on the warm-up lap, but took advantage of his machine's onboard electric starter. This time the Australian made no mistakes and took the race win. Afterwards he was fined Sfr5000 (£2300) for making an 'up yours' gesture at the pit lane.

Bayliss	260 points	9 Wins
Edwards	231 points	2 Wins

Despite being the scene of his first WSB win, in 2002 Colin only managed a third and second at Monza. (Graeme Brown)

'Any other year and maybe I would have been leading the series after Silverstone,' says Edwards, 'but it just wasn't the case, so being behind was the situation I had to deal with. Bayliss had won nine races and I'd won two, but I was still there with him, just 29 points or so behind. You know, that meant one DNF for him, a race win for me and the whole thing would have changed again. I was still right in there.'

By this point in the season, you would have thought that Colin was – to put it mildly – annoyed that he wasn't leading the series. But he wasn't. You could still spot the toothy grin up on the podium and see that he was still enjoying his racing, despite being in Bayliss's wheel tracks. That was because he still believed he was at the height of his powers and riding to the absolute limit.

'Even coming second, it was easy to smile up on the rostrum. That year especially... Despite being behind Troy and Ducati at the time, I felt that the Honda was so much better and so much more consistent. Look at any other year with the Honda and I'd either win or come eighth or ninth or somethin'. But that year I was always up there on the rostrum, so that gave me something to smile about. Also, that season I just knew I was on it. I knew that I was ridin' my ass off and just going better than I ever had at any time in my career... If you give your all and you find yourself second then that's all you can really do. If you ride that hard, and you know you're really going for it, and you can't do any better then what else can you do? I could sit there in second and say I should have won, but deep down I knew I was riding better than I ever had. You have to be satisfied and this was despite the way I'd become years before when anything less than a win was shit. Thing is, while I was riding better than I ever had and doing things with a motorcycle that I'd never done before, so was Troy Bayliss!

'Despite this, after a couple of races I knew it would be a straight fight between us two. On a personal level I knew he was the only guy I was looking at and I was pretty sure I was the only one he was checking out. All I could do was apply the pressure, as he would have done to me. Even at that point, with him so far ahead, I saw he could make mistakes, like at Silverstone.'

The engine cut-out issue would have been more controversial if the final points had been closer. Race one at Silverstone saw Bayliss thunder through the field, and standing water, like a dervish, as if he was convinced he could walk on it. Two crashes showed that he couldn't. But the fact that the bike was still spinning its rear wheel as he jumped up out of the mud and gravel to do battle again raised many eyebrows.

With a 38-point gap going into Silverstone, Edwards knew something had to be done. (Graeme Brown)

Bayliss is down and Colin's on his own to win race one. Bayliss took the second leg. (Gold & Goose)

Surely the thing should cut-out to avoid injuring riders and marshals, and to stop petrol pumping in the event that a fuel line was cut or the tank crushed?

Whatever, Bayliss's fifth place stood and Ducati duly demonstrated that its cut-out system worked for technical man Steve Whitelock. This led to paddock whispers of there being a remote-control device to ensure it worked when it should and didn't work when it was, well, beneficial to Ducati.

Colin never wanted to be involved in any legal FIM (Federation International Motorcycliste, the governing body of motorsport) tribunal wranglings to win the crown – 2000 had given him his fill of that sort of thing. Instead he concentrated on his, and his rival's, riding.

'All I wanna say is hats off to Bayliss. I mean he rode a great race to fall twice and still come fifth that day. I don't wanna say anything about their bike and what was or wasn't working. The thing is our bike has a fuel pump cut out, which is a safety feature... If the bike goes down, the engine cuts out; that's why we have a separate starter on the bike. When I went down on the warm-up lap for race two at Silverstone, the thing just cut out as soon as I was something like 55° leant over. The last thing you want is that thing pumping fuel around if something catches fire after a crash. Hell, it doesn't bear thinking about.'

Indeed it doesn't. Just think back to Kawasaki's Akira Yanagawa crashing out at the Ascari chicane at Monza back in 1998 in a massive fireball. 'Troy's bike was on its side for something like 30 seconds in the first crash and 15 in the second, and neither time did it cut out. That had to be a safety issue. I'm not taking anything away from him, man, he rode awesome on the day, but that shouldn't have happened.'

So what was holding up Edwards in the first half of the season if he was riding so well?

'Well, both Troy and myself had good races and bad races, but for me there was a little inconsistency on the machine front compared with the Ducati. With Troy riding the way he was – and he rode so awesome all season – it was just that little one or two per cent of machine advantage that Ducati seemed to have that made all the difference.'

Edwards believed that the Duke was punchier out of corners than his SP-2, leaving him to play catch up down the straights. He says: 'The Ducati's advantage was that it really accelerated and jumped off the turns well. The thing with the Honda is that, for the first part of the season, we seemed to make a lot of noise coming out of the corners and nothin' else while the Ducatis made a little noise and then accelerated really well. Before Monza I was telling HRC that we needed

10 extra horsepower; after Monza it was like we needed 15! Things were getting critical. We needed that little bit of extra help in this department from HRC. We could have got more outright power from the SP-2 if we wanted, but we didn't want any engine problems. At the start of 2001 we had the same outright power as 2002, but we kept busting engines early on. This isn't any good. You gotta last the race to win it, so reliable power was what we were looking for – and a way to match the Ducatis as they came off the turn.'

Despite Bayliss's nine wins to Edwards's two after the Silverstone round, Colin was buoyed by the fact that he was still pretty close to the Australian on points. 'Even at that point I was confident things would turn around,' he says, 'especially in the four races following Silverstone, at Lausitzring, Misano, Laguna Seca and Brands Hatch. I mean, hey, it's not as if Troy was a million miles away in the points stakes; it was just a margin of 29 points. That's just a race win and a win ahead of Troy and I would have led the championship. Races were coming up now where I was confident we could get on a roll. In 2001 at Lausitzring Troy and I won a race each, so I was confident and comfortable at the circuit, and hoping to claw back some points. The other circuits – Misano, Laguna and Brands – were places that I knew well and knew I could go well at.'

One big fear had to be the thought of the Ducati factory riders Ben Bostrom and Ruben Xaus, and even semi-factory guys like Neil Hodgson, duffing up Colin for points that he would badly need to get back on terms with the Australian. Surely having his own team-mate would have been an advantage?

'I wasn't bothered about not having a team-mate in 2002,' he says. 'In many ways it helped me. It meant that HRC listened to me and me alone when it came down to development of the bike. That helped as the bike became a bit more consistent.'

What also helped is Honda's strong relationship with Michelin. When other riders were resting between races, Edwards was grafting, trying to find the best rubber for his SP-2. 'Man, in 2001 and 2002 I spent so much time bustin' my ass around Michelin's test track. In the first half of 2002 alone I did something like 1,800 miles round there testing tyres while Troy was

enjoying himself at home in Monaco. Then he got to use the tyres I'd picked! The Ducati boys didn't tend to test tyres that much; I did that. What I said kinda went with Michelin that year in WSB, but Ducati still got to use the tyres. I was confident that it would give me an edge on pushing the bike to the absolute limit.'

In the 2002 season alone, Edwards covered a mammoth 12,000 miles on Michelin's test tracks. Little wonder they considered him one of their finest development riders ever.

Despite his confidence both to ride to the limit and break Bayliss's stranglehold on the series it was not to be. Not yet, at any rate.

Round 7 Lausitzring

The two main men in the series were finally joined by a back-to-form Xaus in Germany, although the results were still the same. Bayliss scored a double win, but was pushed to lap-record pace to do it. Edwards, again, scored a brace of runner-up places. He was still in touch, even if he was bored with second place…

Bayliss	310 points	11 Wins
Edwards	271 points	2 Wins

Round 8 Misano

Ducati's backyard brings another double for Bayliss. Yet again Edwards comes second. The only hiccup in an otherwise dominant performance is when Bayliss has to start from the pitlane on his spare bike for the warm-up lap.

Bayliss	360 points	13 Wins
Edwards	311 points	2 Wins

Round 9 Laguna Seca

The perfect time for Edwards to halt the red dominance comes at his home round. Race one sees Edwards lead the way, only to make an uncharacteristic mistake and let Bayliss and Xaus through with four laps to go. He's almost inconsolable. In race two Edwards makes amends with a fine victory, leaving an exciting scrap for second behind him between Bayliss and Hogdson, a scrap which the Aussie eventually wins.

Bayliss	405 points	14 Wins
Edwards	352 points	3 Wins

Lausitz. Another
Ducati double.
(Graeme Brown)

Texan warpaint at
Laguna. Edwards
wanted a double
and the Stars
and Stripes paint
job and lucky Ten
Gallon hat just
might help...
(Graeme Brown)

Champions never give up. Ever. With many – bar the close-knit Castrol Honda team and the Texan himself – considering the season a foregone conclusion, Colin managed to find that little bit extra in race two to salvage a win. This time it was Bayliss's turn to play the bridesmaid. 'Everything just came together and the whole team went from despair to joy. It's about as good as turning points get – after the low point of my season in race one.'

One guy who was watching and couldn't fathom Edwards's self-belief that day was 1993 500cc GP champ Kevin Schwantz. 'I talked to Colin after the first race and he still believed he could do it. I was amazed. I mean, Troy had won somethin' like the first ten races or whatever, but he wasn't going to give up. Later it was even more impressive. Honda told him that he didn't have a job for the next year and that they didn't want him in GPs. He took that and still fought for the series. To take both of those negative things and still come up with a positive is something special.'

Round 10 Brands Hatch

From the outside, this looks like the real turning point. First double win of the year for Edwards on the SP-2 in front of a massive 'home' crowd for the Louth-based Castrol Honda team. If truth be known Bayliss was below par, suffering from a cracked rib courtesy of a practice crash with team-mate Ruben Xaus. The real turning point for Edwards came a week later on 4 August. A third win in the prestigious Suzuka 8-Hour aboard an HRC SP-2 with just that little bit more urgency off the corners than his Castrol bike gave him the lever to get new parts for his regular machine. They would arrive in time for a Michelin tyre test, just before the next round at Oschersleben, Germany.

Bayliss	441 points	14 Wins
Edwards	402 points	5 Wins

The Suzuka 8-Hour bike, which he rode to victory with Daijiro Kato, made his WSB machine 'feel gutless' according to some reports. The improvements to his Castrol bike, along with improved Showa suspension

Victory at home. At last! (Graeme Brown)

Edwards leads Bayliss and Hodgson in race two bidding to stop the Ducati rot. (Gold & Goose)

and new Castrol oil, were small but important. 'The improved engine wasn't actually that noticeable at the Michelin test but when we arrived at Oschersleben the improvement on the previous year was incredible. That first one-hour free practice on the Friday morning was the biggest boost I'd had all year,' says Edwards.

Round 11 Oschersleben

Another soul-less German track, but a second double for Edwards. The obvious differences in his SP-2 were the twin exit pipes for the exhaust system. Suddenly it was Bayliss's turn to play second fiddle – in both races. No one knew how long this would continue.

Bayliss	481 points	14 Wins
Edwards	452 points	7 Wins

The difference between the pre- and post-Suzuka 8-Hour version of the SP-2 had been converted into Edwards's first double win of the season. 'It wasn't at that point that I felt I could win the title but I certainly felt I now had what it took to win every race.' All this meant that the tenth of a second he was losing on Troy Bayliss's Ducati 998F02 in the first half of the season had gone. The boot was on the other foot. But could he really close the gap?

Round 12 Assen

What a difference a year makes. In 2001 this was where Edwards's title defence went sour with two poor tyre choices handing the title to Troy Bayliss. In 2002 it was perhaps where Bayliss felt the pressure of Edwards unrelenting march to more race wins. All that year-long tyre testing was paying dividends, with Colin able to run one compound softer on his Michelins than any of the other French rubber users. Still, all Bayliss had to do was follow Edwards home for the remaining races and he'd win. Easy, right? Race one saw Edwards win from Bayliss to close the points gap on the Australian to just 24. But race two saw the pressure cooker situation get to Troy. He ran off the track at one point, before reeling in the third place battle between Aprilia's Noriyuki Haga and Neil Hodgson. When Haga helped Hodgson into the sand, Bayliss had a safe third place. Instead he fell on the exit of the de Strubben corner and handed

the championship lead, and a Doug Polen-equalling record of seven straight wins, to Edwards.

Edwards	502 points	9 Wins
Bayliss	501 points	14 Wins

Crunch time for both parties. One point separated the two champions. Surely the pressure would mean that anything resembling friendship must be sacrificed on the altar of winning?

'No way,' says Edwards. 'We got on. We'd chat to each other when we saw each other around. He's a super-nice guy; he's no prima donna. He's the same all the time. You'd know what to expect when you spoke to him. His wife Kim is great and he's got good kids so even when he was at the top of the championship beating me every week, I didn't feel too pissed off... I just realised that I needed to start winning them instead.'

Behind every great racer is a great crew chief. Adrian Gorst and Colin ponder the data at Brands Hatch, before the double victory. (Graeme Brown)

Oschersleben was the real turning point. Improved machinery helped Colin to a double. (Gold & Goose)

After another double at Assen, Holland, it came to this. Considering the options at the title showdown at Imola. (Graeme Brown)

Imola: checking
out the opposition
from pole.
(Gold & Goose)

Imola again: race
one in the bag...
(Graeme Brown)

Round 13 Imola

Unlucky for someone, round 13 was to be crunch time. After circling the Earth and completing thousands of miles of racing, practice and testing, it came down to just two 21-lap races of 64.365 miles each to determine who would wear the 2002 WSB crown. With his single point advantage, steam-roller momentum and morale boosting pre-race test before the final round, Edwards looked like the man most likely to win. Bayliss didn't seem to know this, throwing his all into the final races of the year. But, the slight early season advantage had now passed to Edwards and it was Bayliss who had to ride his butt off, just to get second – again – ahead of team-mate Xaus. Race two and the tactics were simple for the Australian. Lead at the slowest possible pace so that team-mate Xaus could duff-up Edwards for second, to leave Bayliss the winner. The points difference would make Bayliss the series winner by just three points. But in race two Edwards wasn't riding for a safe championship. He was revelling in the best form of his life on a bike and tyres that were, effectively, merely an extension of his very being. The final race of the year was a classic. Both men putting in pass after pass on each other. Asking – and receiving – no quarter. Even the fiery Xaus couldn't stomach such a

fight and settled for third. With Xaus dismissed, Edwards still wouldn't settle for anything less than a win – surely nothing more than a feather in the crown. But he was used to riding the scalpel-edge performance of his VTR1000 and took the win from Bayliss by just under a second. But why do it? He could have sat back in third and still won the championship. It didn't fit. For so long he'd done just enough to salvage the points he could, like a true champion, and without crashing. And yet the last few laps you could see he was riding the absolute edge to beat Bayliss. 'I didn't just wanna win the title with a second place. I just had to win it. Nothin' else mattered at the time.'

Edwards	552 points	11 Wins
Bayliss	541 points	14 Wins

From despair at Laguna to delight at Imola and Edwards achieved it all in the most memorable and record-breaking way. It took him nine straight wins to turn a 58-point deficit into a title-winning margin of 11 points. Fans had witnessed the most amazing fight back in the history of two-wheeled motorsport, which, while not round-by-round thrilling, culminated in one of the most highly charged and astonishing final two races of any championship. Ever.

Edwards had bared his very soul in a fightback of such epic proportions. Part of this amazing turnaround must be due to the fact that Colin never gave up. And nor did the team. 'My crew chief Adrian Gorst always had that desire in his eyes. If I ever lost track of what we were chasing I only had to walk in the garage and be reminded of what I was being paid to do,' says Edwards. It must have been tough, as early on in the season Edwards just had to grin and bear it. It shouldn't be overlooked that under the shadow of those nine wins, finishing second while 'busting his ass' effectively gave him the shot at the title, while his machine – the Castrol Honda VTR1000 SP-2 – improved.

But fact can be stranger than fiction. Desperation at the crunch Laguna round made the normally solid and professional Castrol Honda team a little, well, weird. Edwards and his entire team suddenly became superstitious. 'Dude, I had no idea everyone had something goofy going on!' he says. 'I thought I was the only crazy one. I had a beer the night before my Laguna win. From that moment on I made sure I had a beer on the Saturday night of every round – and I've never been superstitious or had a beer the night before. I would also make sure I got a kiss from my wife Alyssia on the front of my helmet. I would wear the same socks, shorts and shirt under my suit all weekend. I would bring one bottle of water to the garage and let Alyssia bring the squeegee bottle. I would zip the sleeves of my leathers to the end then very carefully push them back three or maybe four teeth.'

If you think he sounds crazy, this is what the rest of the team was doing:

Neil Tuxworth, team manager: 'Since Laguna I used the same pen, even though it spilt ink all over my hands.'

Tatia Weston, marketing coordinator: 'I bought a pair of shoes while I was at Laguna Seca and had them on for the Laguna races, and every race after that. I didn't dare wear anything else on race day.'

Adrian Gorst, chief mechanic: 'The cowboy hat I got for Laguna Seca never left my head, I wore it on every day of every round after that winning race.'

Craig Burton, chassis mechanic: 'At Laguna Seca I watched the second race on the big screen in pitlane and Colin won. After that I either watched in the Supersport garage next door or on the pitwall but never in the Superbike garage.'

Simon Stubbs, mechanic: 'I became obsessed with checking the tiny screws on the machine's screen. One came loose around Laguna Seca time and it had been preying on my mind since then. I couldn't help myself.'

Mark Lloyd, engine builder: 'After Laguna I became paranoid about Colin giving me a wink before he left pitlane for the races. I would hold the front of the machine and wouldn't let him go until I got the wink.'

Lindsay Pike, sponsorship coordinator: 'I bought some stars and stripes knickers at Laguna and wore them every race day after.'

Chris Pike, data-logging technician: 'At Laguna Seca I stopped wishing Colin good luck. Every time I said it, he seemed to finish second.'

Chris Herring, PR & marketing manager: 'I made sure I received a text message wishing Colin good luck from my mate Gaz who owns the local Indian restaurant back home. Gaz isn't superstitious but even he got wrapped up in Colin's winning run.'

Mad. Absolutely mad, the lot of them. Edwards says: 'It's amazing that all the team had their own quirky little things going on – and nobody spoke about them until the season was over.' Who cares? It worked.

It helped Edwards to a record-breaking total of 25 podium finishes in one season, beating Doug Polen's 1991 total of 21. Edwards's tally of 25 were also consecutive, beating the previous best of 12 set by Carl Fogarty in two of his four title-winning seasons, 1995 and 1999. Edwards's amazing year easily made him the most successful Castrol Honda rider in a season and meant he had, by the end of 2002, scored 65 podiums in total for the team – just two shy of Castrol Honda's long-serving Aaron Slight. Finally, with 552 points and the championship, he had scored the most points ever in a WSB year. It was a truly amazing fightback in a truly amazing year.

Edwards had shown his quality against Troy Bayliss, another rider at the top of his game. Both brought out the best in each other. Typically, Colin was keen to maximise the team effort involved in such a successful year. 'I do the easy part. I'm doing circles for a living,' says Edwards. 'It's the team I've got to thank. I felt at the time that I was working with probably the best guys in the business and they had all been awesome, all year.'

In the end, it may only have been a two-horse race, but it was one hell of a photo finish.

One of his ex-team bosses watched the whole season with interest. 'I think he has changed a lot since those times with us back in 1995–97,' explains his old Belgarda Yamaha team boss Davide Brivio. 'He is much more mature now, using very well his past experience. I think his strong point is his ability to evaluate situations. If he can't get a win he is happy with second place without doing crazy things. That's why he won the title in 2002. He never gave up, even in the difficult situations. He was always second and Bayliss was continually winning. I believe that not many riders could remain so relaxed and wait for the right opportunity. For sure someone else would have tried to go over the limit to get a win earlier in the season and compromise their title chances. I don't know any weakness in him.'

Ahead of Bayliss in a gripping finale. (Gold & Goose)

To the victor the spoils. A kiss from wife Alyssia. (Gold & Goose)

Getting some serious air time. (Edwards family archive/Jim Press)

whippin'
up a storm

Travelling around the world, working oilfields, Colin Edwards Snr was having a ball.

'Man, I was having a great time, but as is the way of things it came to an end and I eventually settled down. A friend brought his wife's sister over for a vacation, me and Eva got hooked up and we got married. She had a five-year-old son who I adopted in 1972 and Colin junior was born in 1974.'

On 27 February 1974, to be exact.

'We moved around quite a lot,' says Colin Snr. 'We lived in Scotland for a couple of years and had a good life.'

All kids get wanderlust and get up to no good, but there was never a problem finding Colin Edwards Jnr.

'I guess I was about two years old when I would just vanish from the house, without warning,' says Edwards. 'After it happened a couple of times, my mum or dad knew where to find me; they'd go straight to the garage. I'd go into the garage and climb up on my dad's motorbike and they'd find me sitting on the thing making "vroom-vroom" noises. It was inevitable that I would get into bikes. My dad was into motorcycles. Hell, he was motorcycle nuts, so it was a natural progression for me.'

With dad as the gentle driving force, the fledgling biker took to two (well, maybe four at first) wheels.

'Yeah, I was somethin' like three-and-a-half when I got on to two wheels. Dad bought me a bicycle and he took the training wheels off after he'd checked that I could just about wobble off down the street and back without falling off.'

It wasn't long before something with a bit more

Proud dad Colin Edwards Senior with a young Junior. (Edwards family archive/Jim Press)

Christmas Day 1977. That little Suzuki JR50 on the left started it all. (Edwards family archive/Jim Press)

The first tentative steps on a powered two-wheeler weren't done in full protective gear. Kids crash and learn... Dad is in tow behind Junior and the JR50. (Edwards family archive)

poke than just pedal power was required to move things on a little, with Junior getting his first motorbike a few months before his fourth birthday. After all, to breed a champ, it helps if you start 'em young.

'Just after the bicycle, I think it was the Christmas of 1977,' recalls Colin, 'dad bought me a little Suzuki JR50 and that's where it all started. Man, once I had that bike there was no stopping me. It became everything to me that little bike and I wanted to be on it all day, every day. Thing was, where we lived at the time was all built up, you couldn't ride the thing too far. So dad decided to pack up and move to the country where I could have a bit more room to ride my little JR50. We moved to Conroe in Texas and got a place

out of the way with about five acres of land on it. Man, I just rode and rode and rode that little bike. I spent every hour I could on it and God only knows how many times I wore the chain and sprockets out...'

About 44 miles north of Houston, Conroe is a large rural town with a population of around 39,000. Very hot in summer and cool in the winter, this is cattle country with lots of trees, grazing land and rednecks.

With Edwards Snr being big into bikes, it was kind of a natural progression for Colin to become seriously involved in two wheels.

'Dad just loved motorcycles. He messed around with motorcycles,' says Edwards, 'They were a big part of his life.'

And if dad and son got involved in racing, then the whole family had to commit to it.

'My mother, meanwhile, was very supportive,' says Edwards. 'For 11 years, we raced every weekend in motocross and the priority order was where we were going to race, how we were going to eat, when we were going to pay our bills. I didn't know all of that until later. I thought we had lots of money but we didn't have any money until later.'

Playing in your yard on a minibike is one thing, but nothing sharpens your skills like competition. Colin had to go racing if he was to get better and he had to go racing to give a purpose to flying around the yard on a bike.

'First race,' says Colin, 'I was four years old and had been on my little JR50 for a while and I entered a 60cc race. It must have been a helluva sight. This gate full of 60cc dirt bikes, loads of funky little Italjets and stuff and at the end of the gate was this kid on a little JR50. It's funny now, but that's what started all this stuff off.'

An old resumé from 1987, written by Colin Snr and since kept by friend Tom Halverson, makes interesting reading.

'In 1979 I bought Colin an RM-50. He had previously entered a few local races but nothing serious. In late 1979 we retired his JR50 and raced only the RM-50. We were invited to race the PeeWee class in the Astrodome GNC races in March 1980. Hunzikerst, a motorcycle shop in Houston, gave Colin a new stock JR50 for the Dome races. He raced the box stock bike and came in eighth overall. Thus at the age of six he ran his first major race.'

While most mums and dads were worrying about how to clothe their growing kids, Colin Snr had another problem. What to do when Junior outgrew the little 50.

'We kept the 50 for another year or so before dad realised I needed something with a bit more zip,' explains Colin. 'So he bought me a Zinger. He'd get somethin' like three of these things in a crate, buy them for about $900 dollars then go to work on them. It was a little automatic. He'd graft on a YZ60 front end, a QT shaft that wouldn't snap, build linkages and monoshock it with a little nine-inch shock... It was a missile. It did maybe 50mph but it was a pretty vicious little thing. You had to be careful, otherwise it would loop out. Dad had a nine-to-five job, but he did work on these little Zingers. They'd cost him three hundred bucks a piece these Zingers, but after he'd done all that work on them, he'd sell them for about $2850! For one bike! It was painstaking work, but he did a beautiful job on them. He was the man. Pretty soon people knew that if they wanted a Zinger that could win races, they had to go to him. As advertising for his bikes, there I was winning races on my Zinger.'

'I sort of based it all on the dimensions of a YZ60,' explains Colin Snr. A lot of people came up to me and asked where Colin got his bike. When I told them I converted it, that was it, people wanted to buy them.

Flares, sneakers and a short sleeved T-shirt. This kid was tough. (Edwards family archive/Jim Press)

With the JR50 gone, a hand-built (by dad) Zinger was going to take him up to serious competition. (Edwards family archive/Jim Press)

And he was winning on it. A great advert for dad's skills. (Edwards family archive/Jim Press)

They took about three weeks of evenings to build the things.'

Looking back at the old resumé once again adds a little more flesh to Edwards's early results.

'I saw Colin's potential and proceeded to build a modified JR50, which took about six months. In 1981 we prepared for the Astrodome races, and Colin won the PeeWee class. Winning this race, however, was not easy. Competition was tough as he was seven, racing against nine year olds.'

And future great names spotted the kid – and the Zinger – even back then. Fellow Texan Kevin Schwantz remembers seeing young Edwards when he was doing his own dirt riding in the late 1970s. 'I first saw Colin way back in about 1979 or 1980, I think. He had this cool little PeeWee. It looked good. Even then you could see he was good, real good. Years later when he went into road racing I was a bit busy with what I was doing, but I heard what he did over in amateurs in 1991 and that was impressive. It's funny how things work out.'

Edwards's dad, who had also raced in his youth, also remembers just how good his son was from the start. 'He was just so much above everybody else,' he says. 'Even back then I thought that there might be a possibility that he could one day make a living out of it.

Yeah, I guess it was always in the back of my head.'

The resumé lists the major results during the early years: 'GNC Astrodome, 1980, 8th place; GNC Astrodome, 1981, 1st place; GNC Astrodome, 1982, 1st place; GNC Goodtime National, 1980, 2nd place; GNC Goodtime National, 1981, 1st place.'

Meanwhile, Edwards was just enjoying doing what he was doing – racing dirt bikes when most kids were figuring out how to take the stabilisers off their bicycles – but it was tough on finances.

'I didn't know at the time, but my riding was tough on my dad,' says Colin. 'In about 1984–85 all the oilfields went to shit and he was out of a job. He spent his time selling cars just to make ends meet. It was tough. We didn't have a lot of money. Whatever I needed, though, he was there. From 1986 we had a verbal agreement. I'd put in 110 per cent effort and he would handle the financial side of things.'

'When I was on the oilfields,' says Colin Snr, 'I was making decent money, but then in around 1985–86 the oil business took a turn for the worse and I was out of a job. I went from earning more than $100,000 a year to selling cars for cash. Even when Colin got a contract from Yamaha where they gave us bikes and spares and expenses, it was still a struggle. We wanted to go racing

but I had kids and a wife to look after and there I was about 40 years of age and just selling cars to make a living. It was tough. I got in a helluva lot of debt when we were racing. We'd head to a national and I'd put it on a credit card and pay it all afterwards. I always made him responsible for things, too. He always had the option of quitting at the end of every year. We could have gone played golf, baseball, gone fishing or whatever.'

'You see,' adds Edwards Snr, 'I didn't want him to race for me. There were too many PeeWee kids out there racing for their dads. I just asked him to make the decision and if he wanted to put in the effort, I would. But we were also under contract, so I used to tell him every year that he had to make a decision and stick to it.'

Edwards reflects: 'As a kid dad was my best friend. During my racing all the PeeWee dads would hang around together during and after races. They'd chase their kids, worried that they'd fall off and be there to pick up the bike when they did. He didn't. He kinda let me do my own thing. He used to say, "If you can drop it, you can damn well pick it up." Hell, if he had chased me to pick the bike up he would have had a heart attack!'

Senior's seeming indifference bred an independence in Colin that is still part and parcel of the Edwards race armoury today. It was also transparent. Dad cared about his son's racing and wanted to give 110 per cent, even if it meant making big sacrifices.

'In 1985 my dad had this prized possession,' remembers Colin. 'It was a special, a real special, special, that he'd built himself. It had a Rickman chassis with a supercharged V4 motor in it. He'd had this bike ten or maybe 12 years, probably since I was conceived; that's how long he'd had it. He'd even gone to the Isle of Man on it. It was his toy, his baby. It was a real monster. He eventually traded it in at a Kawasaki dealer for two 60cc and one 80cc dirtbikes. That shows you the passion he had for racing and for my career. Thing was that it floated around for a while at the dealers until it was sold. That was a hard thing for him to do, sell that bike. I was just a kid, so I didn't figure that kinda shit out until later, I just saw him trailer the bike away and then come home with three new dirt bikes on the back of the trailer.'

As the young Edwards hit double figures, he'd been riding for more than half his short life, but pretty soon even the Zingers had to go as Colin outgrew them both in physical stature and skill. The kid was good, that much was clear, so hopefully it was only a matter of time before a factory spotted him and would help out.

'I was on a Kawasaki 60 for a while and then got picked up by Yamaha,' says Edwards. 'It was around 1986, I guess, so I was about 12 years old and a factory rider. At the time, from the age of 12 you could ride an 80, so when Yamaha took me on that was what we were aiming at. It was a world away from dad building my bikes himself. Yamaha would give us three bikes a year and all the spare parts we needed for the whole season. Yamaha kind of had a plan… to take me all the way through on the dirt. The guy ahead of me in this 'grand plan' was Damon Bradshaw and they were grooming us both for the future. When I was racing in motocross, I was up against people like Jeff Emig, Damon Bradshaw and Ezra Lusk. These guys are top names now and at the time I was up there with them.'

Factory rider status meant big support from Yamaha, which eased the financial burden a little on Colin Snr.

'We'd get three bikes from Yamaha. One for racing and two for practice – one modified and one stock. One of the bikes was always at home for practice. I won a couple of national championships in 1987, I think.'

During his time with Yamaha, he made a firm friendship. 'Tom Halverson, he was my wrench,' says Edwards. 'He used to spanner my bike in the nationals and we became friends.'

Despite a ten-year age difference between the two, Halverson enjoyed the youngster's company.

'We did a fair bit of horsing around,' remembers Halverson, 'but the big thing I remember is that he was very mature for his age and he wasn't intimidated by anything or anyone.'

And then there was dad.

'Colin Snr wasn't like the other motocross dads.' Indeed he wasn't. Probably more like an Aussie Indiana Jones, with a bush hat in place of the Fedora and the requisite bull-whip. Yes, you read that right, a bull-whip.

'Some of the motocross dads used to drink a lot to relieve the stress of seeing their kids fly through the air,' smiles Halverson. 'Colin Snr used to have this bull-whip, which he was pretty good with. Soon some of the drink made one of the other dads brave enough to get him to whip a cigarette out of his mouth. It was tense, but there was a crack of the whip and a shower

of embers, but Colin did it.'

Away from the track, and even despite the factory backing, things were still tough.

'Throughout all of this, my dad had to find work,' says Edwards. 'He got a job in Dallas and we lived in a duplex – well, tried to live – it was more like a hole in the wall. Things were tough. I didn't know it, but dad was getting deeper and deeper in debt. We were heading towards oblivion.'

Colin Snr did a good job of keeping his son in the dark about how tough things really were, just letting Colin get on with the job of riding, practising and racing. The financial pressures on Colin Snr were matched only by the time pressures on Junior.

'Eventually we moved back to Conroe,' says Edwards. 'We didn't have a track nearby, so to go riding meant a long day. Me and a buddy of mine used to practice every day. I had no car, so I kinda relied on him to get to the track. We'd wake up and then go to school and then ride. We'd ride that much together that I would just leave my bike in his truck. We'd ride for two, maybe three hours a day after school, say from about 4pm to about 6 or 6.30pm. Then we'd get back to his place, clean the filters, wash the bikes and lube the

chains to get the bikes ready for the next day's riding. Then you had to make sure your kit was washed for the next day as well. I'd get home, have some dinner, do a little homework and then bed. I was just 14 years old and there I was working my ass off. The days were so full you didn't even have time to pull your own dick.'

Things were coming to a head, both financially for dad and physically for son. The punishing regime couldn't continue.

'We got to 1988 and I just didn't grow!' says Edwards. 'I was 14 years old, just 80lb and about five feet tall. All the other guys were 120lb and five-five. It wasn't a problem in supercross. I was smooth and no one could touch me. But then we'd get outdoors and I just didn't have the strength to muscle the bike around. We got to the 1988 AMA Nationals at Loretta Lynn's. We got there, did the weekend and when it was all over I just looked at my dad and said, "Man, it's just no fun anymore." I also didn't have time for anything else in my life.'

Colin Snr: 'I think it was something like his first or second year in experts and all the other boys had beards and moustaches and they were killing him, really trying to kill him because he was beating them. That's when

he said that he wanted to pull his option and quit.'

'I was burnt out,' adds Edwards. 'My dad said "Okay, that's cool." I think for him it was a bit of a relief, as he was doing his best to support the family and my racing. I think that it was a relief for all concerned. I was out of the rat race. I went to see Mike Guerra, who was head of Yamaha's race department at the time and just said, "Mike, I'm done. I don't want to do this anymore." I was just so tired with it all. It's strange how things work out, but I think I just started too young. If I had kicked it all off when I was, say, seven or eight, I reckon I would still be racing motocross today. Kicking things off at four was just way too early.'

Time to sell up. 'I pretty much sold the trailer, the bikes, the spare parts, everything as soon as I could,' explains Colin Snr. 'A guy came and picked the lot up. We didn't have a bike in the garage for years after that.'

Even though Colin had quit racing it was still tough to make ends meet in the family.

'Dad was still buying and selling cars,' says Edwards. 'I was about 15 and still at school, but by now I was starting to get into a bit of trouble. It was just the normal stupid shit kids do when they get to that sort of age. Me and some friends started by breaking into

Say cheese! Just the sort of birthday cake a six-year-old bike mad kid should have. But how will the Harley on the cake handle the berms? (Edwards family archive/Jim Press)

Colin and brother Jimmy, who was never far away when bikes were around. (Edwards family archive / Tom Halverson)

Top left: The growing prodigy had to move up to bigger tackle as he outgrew the Zinger. Colin on an air-cooled Kawasaki KX60. (Edwards family archive/Jim Press)

Top right: Mixing riding with school work meant a long day for Colin and the cat. (Edwards family archive/Jim Press)

Bottom left: After the Kawasaki came a factory deal. Riding for Yamaha as part of the company's successful youth programme. (Edwards family archive)

Bottom right: Still in his early teens, he was looking good to move up into the adult motocross ranks, but he was getting burnt out. It was too much, too soon. (Edwards family archive)

houses. I thought we were all having fun, until we got caught one day. That's when it stopped. I figured that it wasn't such fun, as there could have been a guy waiting for me behind a door with a shotgun. It could have turned out very nasty. I also dabbled a bit with drugs. Just the normal shit. Thankfully I didn't like it. I thought it was shit and a waste of my money. I couldn't have afforded to do drugs, anyway.'

Money was still a big issue at home for a teenage boy in Conroe.

'I got a $10 allowance for the week. That was all I had. For a good lunch at school, you had to pay $1.50, but our daily amount for lunch was just one dollar, so to have a good feed you had to make up the shortfall with your allowance. But at last I was getting to be a proper kid. Before I was too busy racing and didn't have time to do the normal shit that kids do, you know, girls and that sort of thing. I was having fun. I was working at Randalls grocery store, stacking groceries for pay. Then I was cleaning up oil spills in a garage. I did anything I could to get money. I realised early on that if you didn't have a bit of money, you didn't have shit. That's why I had a few jobs. My dad had a job at a car lot, so I used to go there and wash the cars for a few dollars, just to get a bit of money together. One year I hacked a few trees down, chopped them into logs and sold them door-to-door. I was kinda lucky, as I was just 16, driving dad's truck around while he drove a loaner from the car lot.'

Pretty soon bikes were to come back into Edwards's life, courtesy of dad again.

'I found a pretty beat up Yamaha FZR1000,' says Edwards Snr. 'I put it back together, got it running and pretty soon, at the age of 16, Colin got his licence and rode it. In fact, I hardly saw it again. I wasn't worried about him, though, as even at that age he was so experienced on two wheels.'

For Edwards it was love at first sight.

'It was a Yamaha FZR1000, one of the early Genesis models. It was so cool. I just looked at it and said, "Fuck!" I had to ride it, so I did a special two-week course to learn to ride it legally and that was it, 16 and riding an FZR1000! I rode it to work, school, man, we just ran around and terrorised the neighbourhood on

that thing. One day, me and a buddy, who had a Suzuki Katana 600, went for a ride. About an hour from my house was this lake, where me and my buddy took a pair of girls. Well, when we started to leave, my bike blew a fuse and I'm left with no lights. So I'm figuring I'm gonna have to ride for an hour in the dark with no lights. I end up taping a flashlight to the front of the bike and off we go. I'm riding about four-feet from my buddy's number plate and I'm bored, so I signal to him that we should go faster. So there we are, doing 120mph, with these girls on the back of our bikes in the pitch black, and only one of them with lights on. Finally, about eight miles from home I finally guessed that maybe I should look in my mirrors to see if there were any cops there. Sure enough I could just make out these little red flashing lights. Shit. So I slow down and gently pull over, hoping the cops will see and chase my buddy, rather than me. After all, I had no lights on. No such luck. They pulled us both over, gave us a ticket each for doing over a hundred miles an hour and then gave me another ticket for having no working lights. Bizarrely, they then let me go to ride home in the dark. Weird. I also ended up with a $240 fine, which there was no way I could pay all at once. So I had to visit the Justices of the Peace to tell them I didn't have the money to pay. I had tried asking my dad, but he quite rightly told me, "I'm not paying that shit… it's your fine." This is where my luck changed for the better. After I'd paid about $60, I visited the JPs office to make another $20 payment, but there must have been some mix up with the records as the JP had changed to another guy. I tried to explain the situation to him, but he just took the $20 off of me and said "Consider the fine paid, son." That was my lucky day, I'd made a $160 saving… on a fine!'

With Edwards loving life back on two wheels, it was only a matter of time before this natural competitor would go racing, even if at the beginning it was only to watch.

'I was just pulling out of the drive with some friends when Colin turned up on the bike,' says Colin Snr. 'He was going riding with his friends and we were going to watch some road racing. He decided to tag along and watch.'

The invite would prove to be a lucky break for Junior.

Colin's style on the TZ250 was smart and neat. (Courtesy Tom Halverson)

the ultimate plan

'I swear, despite quitting dirt racing there was still an ultimate plan in my dad's head. One day in 1990, I saw this Kawasaki, a ZX-7. Man, I wanted one real bad. It was the right and proper colour for a Kawasaki; it was green, blue and white. It was perfect. Anyway, one day I came home and there it was. Dad had bought it for me. Next thing you know, he's saying, "Hey son, let's go to the racetrack." So we get out on the bikes, me on the ZX-7, and we go to the racetrack.'

Colin Snr recalls: 'I was pulling out of the drive with some friends and he pulls up with his buddies. We were off to the racetrack to watch some racing. I told Colin to come along.'

Edwards takes up the story: 'We got there and I could see this guy I used to know. We used to race motocross a few years before and he's out there, doing it, winning races. So I figure, if he can be out there winning, so can I, because I used to beat him off road. I get home, squeeze into my mom's leathers from 1975, get hold of a little Kawasaki Ninja 250 and go out on the track for the first time a little while after that racetrack visit.'

His first time on tarmac was exciting for Colin and probably just as interesting for the bystander to watch. 'I wasn't pretty,' he laughs. 'I was all motocross to begin with, all elbows out and hunched over the front of the bike, but pretty soon I was zipping around the track thinking, "No one can go faster than me on this thing".'

'He was convinced he could beat the other guys,' remembers Colin Snr. 'He did about six laps and came

in, convinced he knew how to go faster and faster. Hell, he didn't even have any knee pucks.'

'That must have been in September 1990,' says Edwards, 'because that's when I got my first road-race licence.'

It had begun. He'd been bitten by the bug, and dad had too.

The pair began taking their first tentative steps towards a full-time shot at road-racing. 'Towards the end of 1990, I kinda showed up at races and used to get the odd ride on other people's bikes. One guy let me ride his Yamaha FZR400 for him and I did a few endurance races towards the end of the year.'

The next year was to be the big one, a full-shot at racing. The old team of Colin Edwards Snr running the show with Colin Edwards Jnr riding returned after a few years kicking back. Edwards felt the time was right.

'Dad and I decided to sell the ZX-7 and FZR and go racing full-time in 1991,' says Edwards. 'I guess it was time for me to do something; I was 17 and didn't want to waste all those years of two-wheeled experience. I'd raced from the age of four to 14, so I guess the intervening years were just me having some time off. With the money we got for the bikes, dad and I bought a Honda CBR600. He had to get a bit of finance to back us up to buy the bike. It was a race bike, but it was only a production-tuned machine, so it was fairly close to standard. The plan was this: I was to run the bike in A, B and C class races. Despite only just starting this tarmac racing, I found that at the beginning of the year I was undefeated and in a few events I was actually beating some of the guys who were rated as experts. Maybe I was getting the hang of it.'

Maybe he was. Money was still tight, though, and any help towards running costs was welcomed. Consumables such as chains, tyres, brake pads and fuel cost money, any product sponsor or way of getting the kit for free would help.

'Around this time I met a guy called Ronnie Lonsford,' says Colin. 'Ronnie was running a bike shop and he could see that I was winning races. At the time Dunlop was supplying a set of tyres for the winner of each race, so Ronnie loaned me a standard bike, which meant I was running in six out of the 15 races in a weekend and winning six sets of tyres...'

Time and money were running out, though, for Colin Snr.

'Going to Willow Springs that year was crunch time,' he says. 'We didn't have the right size trailer, so I bought a box trailer and a Ute on credit. I remember thinking to myself, "If someone doesn't spot him this time we're going to have to shut this thing down".'

He didn't have to worry. Edwards the novice equalled the professional lap record that weekend and went out and beat a rider on a trick Erion/Two Brothers Racing machine. This startling performance got him noticed by Eric Klemintich, a road-racing enthusiast of the old school and a man who put his money where the talent was.

'Eric was a mega enthusiast,' says Edwards. 'He said he wanted to help me out. He asked me if would I like to travel to all the AMA national events and endurance events using a kitted Honda RC30 superbike. He also had a 1991 Yamaha TZ250 two-stroke, which I also rode in some club races. So now I was running in eight of the 15 races, but still a novice. This meant that I started in the second wave of riders. I won all of my novice races and even two of the races overall by coming through the second wave and then the first wave riders to take the overall victory. All this was happening at the same time as all the normal stuff. I was a junior in high school, but I was also travelling to Minnesota, New Hampshire, Dakota, to enter all these races; and travelling… in a

ratty old van with an RC30 stuck in the back. At the end of 1991 I entered eight classes in the WERA finals and won all eight. Then at the AMA finals I won five out of the eight races. The three I didn't win, I was in the second wave (still a novice) and had trouble fighting through the other guys. All in all it was a good year, as I won 13 titles in a two-week period.'

Colin Snr remembers it well: 'He was riding against guys with 1100 or 1200 GSX-Rs on his four-stroke 600. I still reckon that if he could have used the 250 against them they wouldn't have seen which way he went.'

With such a record against the amateurs, it was only natural that Colin should try to get bumped into the pro racers' pool as soon as possible. It was essential for him to do this quickly so that he was up against the sort of opposition that would bring him on even further.

He eventually made it to pro in his first full season of racing, finally turning professional in November 1991 and finishing second in his 250cc national debut at Miami in the last race of the season.

'Yeah, as well as the 600 I was riding the 250 too, don't forget. By the end of 1991 I wanted to get a pro licence so I could take on the big boys at an AMA race at Miami. I wanted to take on the likes of Jimmy Filice and Rich Oliver. These were the guys to beat and I figured I had to race them to improve. I ended up asking for a provisional pro licence. It was strange, as you needed something like 300 points for a pro licence but despite having something like 400 I was only allowed to have a provisional licence. Either way I took part in the pro race and ended up finishing second to Jimmy Filice, which for a newly turned pro, or provisional pro, was pretty good going. It was about this time that I hooked back up with Tom Halverson, my old wrench from my motocrossing days. I was at a race watching the pros go out and I spotted him just sitting there on the ground. He was doing someone's split-times or whatever. I asked him what the hell was he doing with himself and pretty soon after that he came to help me out on the 250.'

Tom remembers: 'I was scouting for Yamaha at the time. I think it was Road Atlanta when I spotted them. I recognised Colin Snr from the big Australian hat he always wore, but next to him was this tall guy I didn't recognise. It was Colin, who'd grown about two feet since I last saw him.'

The year 1991 was a stellar first year for Colin. He reels off the results matter of factly, but you cannot imagine the impact his results had. In his first year of racing, as an amateur on a 600 Honda, a Honda RC30 and a Yamaha TZ250, he won every race he finished. He was unbeaten in his amateur career, winning a record five national titles in the AMA/CCS Race of Champions at Daytona and a record eight national titles in the WERA/GNF meeting at Road Atlanta. All this marked him out as special. Very special.

'That sort of thing didn't happen often,' says Halverson. 'And you have to remember, at the time there were a lot of good kids out there. You could see he had so much raw talent off the bat. I knew he would be dangerous when he got going.'

That year was also a very special year for another reason – Colin met Alyssia Henson the girl he would later marry.

'I met Colin just as he was getting into his racing seriously,' says Alyssia. 'I was about 16 or so, I guess. That makes us childhood sweethearts. I'd just split from my last boyfriend and a mutual friend of mine asked if there was anyone around I kinda liked, so I told her that Colin was pretty cute. Eventually, he asked our mutual friend about me and it went from there.'

As is usual in such situations, the course of true love never runs smoothly. Especially when one of you uses chewing tobacco, the only remnant of Edwards's youthful and half-hearted dalliances with drugs.

'When we first met, he was so sneaky about it,' says Alyssia. 'He even kept his stash hidden from me for six months after we met. He used to swill his mouth out before I came round or before he came to see me. But I guess I got hooked on him before I found out he was a dipper. That's what we call people who use that stuff, as you have to dip it under your lip by your gum. He's quit a couple of times, but seems to get back into it when he's had a bad race, because he knows I'm not going to rip into him then. I know who gives it to him as well. It's those suspension guys from Öhlins. They get all the Swedish chewing tobacco stuff. I call them the paddock pushers…'

Many journalists will tell you that the first time they interviewed Colin was a little disconcerting. Not because he was difficult to interview, just that he'd often pause between questions so he could spit into a Coke can, plastic cup, anything that he could spit into. Unless you were an American and used to such practices, you'd think he was ill and about to be sick.

Sitting next to Colin during dinner at the launch of his 1997 Yamaha team with co-rider Scott Russell, the author was forced to ask about the Texan's habit. He'd sit and talk to you, easy-going, good company, but always spitting into whatever receptacle he could find. His wine glass, your wine glass, whatever.

'Dude, don't knock it till you've tried it,' he said, producing a tub of the stuff and proffering it to me.

I'd dined on Yamaha's free corporate hospitality and despite being a confirmed non-smoker, I thought, 'What the hell'.

I dipped into the tub, took a large lump of tobacco and stuffed it in my mouth, easing it down between my cheek and gums.

Nothing happened for a few minutes then I was greeted by a huge nicotine rush that saw my mouth turn into Niagara Falls. I couldn't stand, let alone talk. I spat in my wine glass. Colin thought this was funny. Hilarious, even. Then, Russell, learned sage that he is, came over to me, wagging a finger, warning, 'Hey, don't you go becoming a big dipper…' When I'd recovered, Colin gave me several tubs of the stuff, which unsurprisingly remain unused to this day.

'The winter of 1991 was an exciting time for me,' says Edwards. 'Tom had agreed to help me on the 250, my dad had started a team and Eric had come up with the money to run us. Yamaha also supplied the bikes and I had my first team-mate, Chris Dalusio. I figured it was going to be pretty tough for me as Chris was a bit of a veteran and, along with Filice and Oliver, was considered to be 'the man' on a 250. I thought that it was going to be a learning year for me, kinda doing things properly and with a good, experienced team-mate to learn from. In the 250 class that year, I would also come up against Kenny Roberts Junior, who, like me, had the opportunity to ride bikes from when he was a kid, even if it was a bit less of a struggle than it

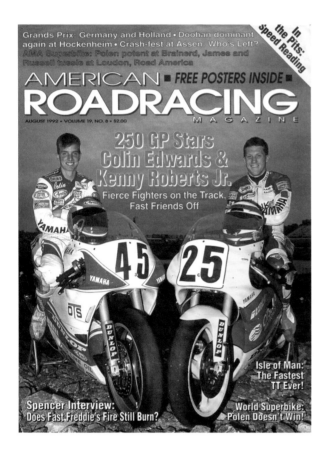

Grands Prix: Germany and Holland • Doohan dominant again at Hockenheim • Crash-fest at Assen: Who's Left?

AMA Superbike: Polen potent at Brainerd, James and Russell tussle at Loudon, Road America

In the Pits: Speed Reading

AMERICAN ■ FREE POSTERS INSIDE ■
ROADRACING MAGAZINE

AUGUST 1992 • VOLUME 19, NO. 8 • $2.00

**250 GP Stars
Colin Edwards &
Kenny Roberts Jr.**
Fierce Fighters on the Track.
Fast Friends Off

Isle of Man:
The Fastest
TT Ever!

Spencer Interview:
Does Fast Freddie's Fire Still Burn?

World Superbike:
Polen Doesn't Win!

*American
Roadracing's
front cover during
the AMA 250 GP
season hit the
nail on the head.
Two Juniors but
only one winner.
(Courtesy
Tom Halverson)*

had been for me and my dad. The first race in 1992 was the AMA season opener at Daytona in Florida. I won the 250 race, with Chris second, which was a helluva result for the team.'

Winning his first 250 race made him the target of journalists in the pitlane. Perhaps one of the first interviews he gave came after winning the race. Paul Carruthers, son of legendary two-stroke tuner and racer Kel, was editor of *Cycle News*, the prestigious American motorcycle paper, and he knew that Edwards was marked out for greatness.

'I actually interviewed Colin for a story in *Cycle News* the day after he won. It was his first ever interview. At the time he came across as a nice kid with a good family, and nothing's really changed. He was one of those kids that you knew was going to make it big. He rode well and he had his head together and, of course, there was tons of talent. What's nice about Colin is the fact that he's never changed. He didn't change when he started winning races over here, and he hasn't changed since becoming world champion. I can still pick up the phone and call him and talk about anything. He's also one of those guys who cares about you and what you think. He even asks about my family when I talk to him; not many racers bother with things like that. As far as interviewing goes, Colin is the best. He tells you what's on his mind and there's no bullshit involved. He's the real deal.'

In 1992 Edwards should have had a year of slow learning from his experienced team-mate Dalusio. This was the year things should get tough for the 18-year-old rookie. He was a pro, but in a bigger pool of more experienced riders. Many thought this would prove to be the kid's comeuppance. It didn't.

'Despite me being the rookie in the team and being expected to learn off of Chris,' says Edwards, 'I ended up winning five of the nine races in the championship that year and became the AMA 250 champ. Second overall was Kenny junior.'

National champ in his first pro year and he was still at high school.

It wasn't all plain sailing for Edwards, though. Racing motorcycles means crashing motorcycles and that leads to injury. Over the years Colin has been lucky.

'Pretty much. Before 1997 and my big crash at Monza, I'd only done the wrist, elbow and collarbone, all on the left-hand side. They didn't give me pain, but I only had limited movement in the wrist.'

The wrist was a result of a 1992 crash on his 250 when he realised he had no brakes and hit an Armco fence.

'I was lucky I only broke the wrist that day,' says Edwards. 'It all happened when I came out of the pits at Texas World Speedway, through the long, long left-hander. The following corner is a 90° right-hander. So I came into there, down through the gears, started pumping the front brake. But it was like, oh, no pressure. There was a hole in the brake lines, so I just had to lay it over and ended up with the wrist injury. I didn't know it at the time, though, as I raced the next day. In fact, it went on like that for a month as I just didn't know it was broke. It was the scaphoid and it hurt like hell. I went to Brainerd and won, but it hurt bad so I got it X-rayed and had surgery. They put two screws in it and three weeks after the surgery I won at Mid-Ohio.'

As well as helping Colin in the 250s, Halverson was working for Vance & Hines, one of the biggest teams in the AMA Superbike championship and effectively the factory team for Yamaha. Edwards's dominance in the 250 class had certainly caught their eye.

'People were thinking "this kid is really good",' recalls Halverson. 'In fact, at the end of 1992 we went to an All-Japan race at the Fuji circuit, just to get him noticed. He was on a pretty stock TZ250 when all these Japanese Yamaha guys were on trick factory TZ-Ms. Tetsuya Harada, the champ that year, was racing. I don't remember where Colin finished, but he impressed.'

Colin seemed to be two-stroke bound, with a national title to his credit. Why didn't he go to 250 GPs? Colin Snr explains: 'There was just no opportunity for us and we had no money. We had an option to go into the European Open series with Kenny Roberts Snr, but again we didn't have the money.'

Another two-stroke team showed an interest. Cagiva.

'It was about midway through 1992 when American Ducati team owner Eraldo Ferracci came to us and tried to get Colin to sign a contract for $100,000 to ride in GPs the following year for Cagiva.

Halverson and Colin at Fuji for an All-Japan 250 race. (Courtesy Tom Halverson)

Off he goes on the TZ250 at Fuji in front of the cameras (Courtesy Tom Halverson)

Taking some time out with dad...
(Courtesy Tom Halverson)

Every inch the new, young kid on the block, Colin was a fresh-faced youngster when he came on the scene in AMA Superbike in 1993.
(Gold & Goose)

...and with the ladies in Japan.
(Courtesy Tom Halverson)

He was still contracted to Yamaha and they had first refusal on him for 1993 so I said we'd sign a letter of intent only at the end of the year when we could see how things turned out. We were supposed to go to the Superprestigio event to test the Cagiva, but the week before Mat Mladin tested it and was signed.'

It wasn't a case of worrying about what could have been. Colin Snr and Junior didn't work like that, although the thought of the 19-year-old Edwards lining up alongside Rainey, Schwantz, Doohan et al on the improving Cagiva was a mouth-watering one.

'He never let that get to him,' says Colin Snr. 'One of his strengths is his ability to see the big picture and accept what happens will happen for the best.'

But in motorcycling lives can be fragile.

'About three-quarters of the way through the 1992 season, a friend of mine, Larry Schwarzbach, died, which unfortunately meant there was a spot on the Vance & Hines team for 1993,' says Edwards. 'I ended up getting a ride with them on a two-year deal, along-side Jamie James on the new YZF750.'

Jamie was the 1989 champion, riding a Suzuki GSX-R750, so even back then he was very experienced. Unfortunately a severe hand injury forced him out of the first two races of the year.

The season started well enough for Colin, taking fourth place behind Scott Russell. Doug Polen's Ducati 888 and his returning WSB Fast by Ferracci crew made the event their own. Doug wanted to win the AMA title pretty badly to add it to his back-to-back WSB titles.

At the second race of the season – the prestigious Daytona 200 – James's replacement was one Eddie Lawson.

For many, including the Vance & Hines crew (despite a DNF for Colin), the 1993 Daytona was a special event, as Lawson took his second Daytona win. If Edwards was disappointed, at least he'd played a small part in Lawson's victory, as recounted by Jim Leonard to American journalist Dean Adams. And all this was achieved despite some reliability worries with the ageing Yamaha FZR750R, better known as the OW-01. The OW was used by the team for the first few rounds of the AMA series that year before they got up to speed with the newer YZF.

In 1993 during the first few rounds, the elderly OW-01 was used while the new YZF was being prepared by the Vance & Hines team. (Gold & Goose)

The new YZF750SP came on stream midway through the 1993 season. Colin would get to know it well over the next four seasons... (Gold & Goose)

'We worked really hard in the winter to get not only more power but better acceleration from the bike,' Leonard said to Adams a few years after the race. 'We did that by making a lot of combustion chamber changes and porting the heads, and we picked up a substantial power increase. The problem was, as we made the engine more efficient, we didn't have an adjustable ignition. This meant that we were running too much advance, and when we got to Daytona we were overheating and blowing up engines left and right. I was literally building engines in the garage at Daytona with the bottom end from this one and the top end from that one, and grinding off parts and clearancing things, and struggling and struggling.'

Interestingly, that day 'Steady' Eddie set an example for Edwards for the future, one that would become almost part and parcel of the Texas Tornado's future racing psyche. Lawson simply rode around the problems and never lost his focus during the race, even

when it was thought he could not win the event.

With practice meaning engines were blowing up left, right and centre, Eddie was sent out for the race on the last engine that was left over. The team simply guessed the jetting settings and sent the Californian on his way. Although it wasn't considered so at the time, Edwards's retirement to the pits during the race was a silver-lining for the team, as he effectively left a pair of scuffed tyres sitting on his bike, which the four-times GP champ would need before the end of the race.

'I'm not sure if we would have won or not if Colin hadn't dropped out, because we did an extra stop,' explained Leonard. Instead of the two pit stops most riders chose, Lawson came in three times.

'Eddie and Scott Russell were really going at it head-to-head. Before the last stop, I really thought about the tyres. I thought, if I put him on a new tyre he was gonna lose so much time on the out lap, Scott was gonna kill us. So I grabbed one of Colin's scuffed

tyres. It was a different tyre, on a different width rim, but it was scuffed. So I threw it on the bike on Eddie's last stop. On the out lap, we gained over a second on Russell.'

Lawson went on to win the 200 over Russell in an amazing last lap draft pass coming towards the finish line.

'I asked Eddie in the winner's circle, "How about that last tyre?",' says Leonard. 'He looked at me and said, "The last tyre was spinning in fifth gear on the banking". When he said that I was thinking, this is not good. But then he smiled, and said, "It was bitchin". That was pretty cool. A magical experience.'

Lawson was famed for his work-rate, compared with a more naturally talented racer of his era, such as Freddie Spencer, and for his skills at evaluating the opposition, the track, the tyres, the bike and himself. It's a skill spookily reminiscent of Edwards now, at the height of his powers.

Round two at Laguna Seca saw Doug Polen come through from tenth on the first lap to win the race. It was to be a theme for the year as the returning WSB champ took his 888 and team back home to claim the title. The next round saw Edwards show some promise at Tobacco Road in North Carolina. It's a high-speed circuit with little run-off, which would scare the bravest of road-racers. Makeshift wooden chicanes slowed things down a little, but there were still two red flags during the race. Second place went to Edwards on the old FZR. At Road America Edwards got hold of the new YZF750SP and put it on pole position. He was 19 and full of confidence compared with the old-timers. Edwards figured on breaking Polen's almost mythical dominance by simply going like hell during the first few laps. It worked at first. By the end of the third lap he was four seconds ahead of Miguel DuHamel's Kawasaki and a further seven ahead of Polen. But by lap four Pascal Picotte – Polen's team-mate – had

Cool as ever,
before the season
opener at Daytona
in 1994. (Edwards
family archive/
Tom Halverson)

Dietary habits left
something to be
desired in the
early days!
(Gold & Goose)

moved into second past DuHamel and Polen behind was catching too. With two laps left, Polen took the lead. Call it youthful exuberance, but Colin didn't want to let the old hand go. The result was a collision with Picotte. Both went down and both got up pointing fingers at each other.

It may have been then that his frustration with twin-cylinder bikes and riders set in. At the time Colin said: 'You feel like you're beating yourself before you go out there. You don't want to think Ducati has an advantage, but it does. Don't get me wrong, Polen's a good rider, but personally I think the bike needs some weight added to it. I got a good drive out of turn one and he pulled seven bike lengths on me. It was all over. Go figure.'

It would be three races down the line before Colin would get another top ten finish (fourth at Brainerd) that would kickstart some results towards the end of the season. Eventually, he finished behind Takahiro Sohwa's Kawasaki in the championship, two places behind team-mate James.

For Edwards, sixth place overall in his first AMA Superbike year wasn't anything to write home about, despite it being his rookie year on the big bikes.

'I guess I had some good races and some bad races,' he says. 'I got a couple of seconds and thirds but nothin' special. At least I didn't think it was anything special.'

In 1994 he was in his second year on the big super-

bike, but things didn't work out until towards the end of the season.

The year saw two noted Australians come to the series to play – Troy Corser and Kevin Magee. Kevin was a legend. A 500cc GP winner, the Australian veteran was joining the Martin Adams-owned Smokin' Joe's Honda outfit, armed with the new V4 RC45. Troy Corser was the 1993 Aussie Superbike champ. He, like Colin, had cut his teeth on a 250, albeit a Suzuki production machine. But, at 22, Troy was two years older than Edwards and already had a national championship under his belt. He was also armed with the formidable Fast by Ferracci Ducati 888, which was in its final year of front-line racing.

Edwards and Jamie James remained on the Vance & Hines YZF750SPs.

Daytona was the season's first round. Scott Russell took his Muzzy Kawasaki to the win on his regular season opener before heading to Europe and WSB, chased all the way by Corser on his Ducati. After 200 miles of hard racing, Dukes weren't supposed to be that strong. Lawson was third, back from Indy Lights again, and riding a very special YZF straight from Japan.

At Phoenix International Raceway in Arizona Corser went one better and made his debut win. Edwards managed to make up for his poor Daytona with a third place. Pomona saw Corser win again. The AMA rookie was proving to be a worthy replacement for Ferracci's

Colin was soon finding the limit on the YZF...
(Gold & Goose)

Colin lines up for the start of the 1994 Daytona 200. (Gold & Goose)

previous rider, Polen, who had been lured by big Yen over to the fledgling Castrol Honda team in WSB. Edwards began a mid-season losing streak, crashing out on his own oil while lying third.

At Laguna Seca, Corser's team-mate, Picotte, took the victory, as Edwards's poor luck continued when he crashed out on oil left by Thomas Stevens's exploding Yoshimura Suzuki. Picotte followed up this win with another at Road America, despite urgent new rules that saw around 10kg (20lb) added to the weight of the twins. Corser made good again at Loudon in New Hampshire. Then, finally, Edwards's season got into gear.

'Yeah, it wasn't until about three-quarters of the way through that season that I decided to pull my finger from my ass and start riding. It all started when I was midway through the 1994 season. I realised that I wasn't getting what I wanted, not achieving all the goals I had set myself. So I was sittin' there with my brother watching TV; it was kinda late, as he used to work until 10pm. So late was the only time we could bullshit. On the TV this guy is talking about these tapes, subliminal tapes. Tapes that can motivate you or something as you sleep. I thought that as I had nothing to lose I'd order myself one and see what happened. Before listening to the tape the instructions said things like, "identify your goals before you start". I guess to me that was pole position, the lap record and a race win. That's what I wanted. So I went to sleep and played the tape.'

At the next race, Mid-Ohio, Edwards did just that. He secured pole position during qualifying and then went out and won the race on Sunday, taking with it the fastest lap, which was a new lap record. It was the talking point of the race.

Better still for the team, he was followed home by his team-mate James, who was challenging Corser and Picotte for the title. One team that was out of the chase was the Smokin' Joe's, with Magee becoming increasingly frustrated by the hard-to-turn RC45s. Meanwhile, Edwards was honest, saying that the tapes helped, as did a refined set-up on his YZF750.

Halverson reckons it was just a trick to put the Ducati's mythical dominance out of his mind. 'The Ducatis at that time had a lot of speed and little weight. I think he wanted to have the confidence to

beat the Dukes, and maybe he got the edge from what he did. Then, when he realised he could do it, beating them gave him another edge.'

It was the start of a phenomenal run. He won again at Brainerd, recognised by many as a classic race and one of the best in AMA history, with no less than eight riders going for the win. An important first act was DuHamel's performance on the Harley-Davidson VR1000. He managed fourth on the lump of Milwaukee pig-iron. But for a last-lap slide it could have been so much better, but it was Edwards who won a dramatic race by seven tenths of a second, ahead of Corser with James beating the French Canadian's Harley. Corser was lucky to be racing after rolling a hire car on the Thursday before the race on the track and then badly injuring his right hand in a practice crash.

On the same day as Brainerd, the V4 RC45 won its first major international race at the Suzuka 8-Hour endurance event in the hands of the factory's WSB stars, Aaron Slight and Polen, ahead of Kawasaki's Russell and Terry Rymer. It proved to be the closest race in the event's 17-year history, with Slight edging out Russell by just 0.289 seconds. It also proved to be Eddie Lawson's last ever motorcycle race.

Back to the AMA and Corser's lead in the series completely evaporated at Sears Point. The Aussie was battling with Edwards's YZF when the frame on his 888 cracked near the shock linkage, making the bike bottom out and high-side the 22-year-old out of his seat. Edwards won, with James third. Edwards's team-mate now led the series by three points with just one race remaining.

The last race of the season was at Mid Atlanta and Scott Russell, the reigning WSB champion, showed up on his WSB Muzzy Kawasaki to do battle.

Edwards out-did Scott for pole, but there was no toying with the Georgian in the race. No one saw which way he went and he won by ten seconds. Behind him was where the action took place. As Russell completed his disappearing act, Edwards slowed things down to allow his team-mate, who was battling at the back of a pack for third position, to catch up. Jamie got the hint and put a spurt on to take second place, passing Corser, Picotte and Dave

Try as he might, getting on a par with the dominant Ducatis was difficult in 1993/94. (Gold & Goose)

Despite being one of the youngest riders on the AMA circuit, by the end of 1994 Colin was the class of the field. (Gold & Goose)

Sadowski. On lap 20, though, things went sour for Vance & Hines Yamaha. James's EXUP exhaust valve stuck and he dropped back to eighth (seventh after the Harley VR1000 dropped out with a broken fuse.) It wasn't enough, as Corser passed Sadowski to finish fourth, the extra point making all the difference.

It was sad for the team, but Edwards had come good at the end of the season, just when it mattered and finished fifth overall in the championship.

He was looking good for 1995. He'd finished strongly and had a contract in his pocket to stay with Yamaha USA for the next two seasons.

His meteoric rise was noticed by Yamaha staff across the globe, as future team boss Davide Brivio recalls.

'There was a guy who worked for Yamaha and he told me at the start of 1993 that there was a promising young rider racing in the US,' says Davide. 'So I checked and tried to get more information about him.'

'I was just looking forward to staying in the US,' recalls Edwards. 'And I was looking forward to winning the AMA Championship. Then Yamaha said they were putting together a WSB team and would I want to go there. They said it was to be a real world effort, with Yamaha Europe paying for the team, Yamaha USA paying me and Yamaha Japan paying my team-mate's wages.'

'I wanted him to stay with us,' says Halverson, 'because things were looking good for the next year. He was Vance & Hines' future, but I also pushed for him to go, as I knew it was going to be good for him.'

Decision time and Edwards's answer was typical Colin.

'I said, "What the fuck. Let's go".'

The Texas Tornado was about to hit the world stage.

Brands: a rider's
circuit Edwards
would continue
to do well at
in the future.
(Gold & Goose)

a cockroach called colin

The small Japanese cockroach is an interesting specimen, as it contains pheromones that make it more attractive to the opposite sex. That wasn't why Carl Fogarty trapped one in a jar, it was just that the reigning World Superbike champion was bored in his hotel room at the Sugo round of the 1995 season. Calling it Colin just seemed like the right thing to do.

Edwards and Carl had not got off to a good start. Foggy had claimed that in 1995 Colin was one of the first people to say that he couldn't win on anything other than a Ducati and that if he was riding a four-cylinder machine, the result would be completely different. Perhaps the naturally combative Foggy race psyche needed a nemesis close at hand, someone to rail against. It had happened before, with Muzzy Kawasaki's Scott Russell in 1993, the American's

championship year, then again in 1994 with Castrol Honda's Aaron Slight.

Two Vietnamese pot-bellied pigs, Scott and Aaronetta, back home in Blackburn, were testament to Foggy's taste for calling animals by his rivals' names.

But they were pets, of a sort, while a cockroach is, well, a pest – something you do your best to destroy. At the time, Colin was none too pleased to hear that such a creature was named after him.

'Yeah, he says he has a cockroach called Colin. Pretty fucking sick, huh? I guess that's his way of motivating himself to do well. You get stuff like that in football. I understand that, it's human nature. It's great for the entertainment. As long as he can take it I'll dish it out as well. Actually we were kind of friends, I thought, at the beginning of the season. Then he said I

Colin arrived in the World Superbike paddock for the first round at Hockenheim. Dad came too... (Gold & Goose)

He's 'avin a larrfff. The start of the season and Colin sets his stall out early. Larking around with team-mate Nagai. (Gold & Goose)

He'd worked with legends such as Eddie Lawson and John Kocinski, now he was with Colin. Fiorenzo Fanali tries to get inside his rider's head. (Gold & Goose)

was bitching about Ducati and if he was as slow as I was he'd wait until he got some results before mouthing off. Fuck, I couldn't care what he says.'

Fogarty's beef, as revealed in his autobiography, was that he felt Edwards was just a bit too quick and vocal with his comments on the age-old WSB debate of Ducati and twins versus the four-cylinder machines of Honda, Kawasaki and Yamaha. It was probably understandable considering the battles he'd had with Polen and Corser on the rocketship 888s in AMA. But as Carl recounts in his book, *Foggy – The Autobiography*: 'The Texan was another rider who I didn't like that year. He had come over here for the first time and was one of the loudest to shout his mouth off about me and the Ducati. I told him, "If I was as slow as you are I'd wait until I could beat my own team-mate before I started gobbing off".'

At the time, Edwards couldn't remember what or if he had actually said anything derogatory about Fogarty on the twin.

'You know what the thing is, I couldn't actually remember doing any bitching about Ducati,' says Edwards. 'I mean they were winning all the races so everyone was bitching about them and the rules. Yeah, the Fogarty deal is funny. I will say if there is no Ducati, there's no Fogarty. He's a good rider, sure. He's won every fucking race this year, but he didn't do it without Ducati.'

Either way, each verbal spat fanned the flames and made good copy for sensationalist weekly newspaper *Motor Cycle News*, back in the UK. Years after, with hindsight and a more mutual respect for each other, the change between the two was obvious.

In his last year of racing, 1999, on the podium after another race win, Carl was asked by interviewer Suzi Perry, 'When are you going to quit racing, Carl?' To which Fogarty nodded towards Edwards and said, 'When this bloke starts beating me every weekend.'

For Edwards, 1995 was a new venture. He'd been expecting to stay in the AMA series for another two seasons, to hone his racecraft and win the AMA Superbike title. Yet here he was, after just four years of riding a road-race machine full-time, up against the

best four-stroke racers in the world. It was another wake-up call. One advantage he had over some American racers who took the plunge abroad was that he'd travelled across Europe before, so he was no redneck abroad (unlike Scott Russell, who in his early years abroad only ever took dollars with him).

'All the travelling wasn't really a problem,' says Edwards.' When I was younger I travelled round the world a few times; it was just something that had to be done to do the job.'

'In 1995, from round one at Hockenheim until Salzburg, I stayed in Italy, near the team in a hotel. That was no fun, although I made a lot of friends in Italy and pretty much everywhere Alyssia and myself had people we enjoyed hanging out with. I enjoyed the first year on the road and was really happy to be in Europe. As far as getting used to the different continent, I think the best advice about coming to Europe I got was from Kevin Schwantz or Wayne Rainey – I'm not sure which one it actually was now. He said, "As long as you accept Europe for what it is, and don't try to bring a

little of America over there, then you will be fine. Accept the food for what it is, and just do as the Romans do." And they were right. We loved it, and Alyssia got a taste for Italian food.'

But the time spent in a hotel, despite making friends, meant that they needed their own little home on wheels in 1996. 'I wanted to have a home on the road, so towards the end of 1995 I bought a Gulfstream, which I thought would be pretty comfortable. Thanks to buying the motorhome, I more or less had a second family in Biggin Hill, England. They took care of my motorhome and I stay in touch with them all the time. They came to our wedding in the States and the whole nine yards. We've got a really good base with them, and we're great friends as well.'

Strangely, the jump from the AMA paddock to the WSB paddock wasn't such a big deal for Colin. AMA Superbikes in the mid-1990s was a fairly well-funded, well-organised series. It had a pool of talent where, strangely, many riders didn't actually make the jump from national to international status. Some, such as Miguel DuHamel and Doug Chandler, had done it all before and were happy enough to count the championships and the dollars that came with them. But it was a big series, an important series even compared with the (still growing) WSB championship. So the all-important barometer of a championship's success – size of the team transporters, hospitality units, etc. – meant there wasn't much in it between the two series. Yet.

'Yeah, when I first went to the WSB paddock it was a bit of a shock. I mean, at the time, when I went to a GP paddock, I'd feel the atmosphere immediately. It was electric. In World Supers I just didn't feel it at first. I went to Laguna with my brother and friends and we walked into the paddock on the first day and it was like "Where's everybody at? Is this the whole show? It looks like an AMA race!" It just didn't have the electricity. I'm one for pressure. It seems to motivate me more. This is a world championship, so you expect some feeling that you're participating in a big event, but it seems to be missing some.'

The season itself was one of ups and downs and an ultimate low for Colin and the team.

The team set-up was a factory one, but based at

Round one at the power circuit of Hockenheim and Colins junior and senior join the team during practice to check the timing screens. (Gold & Goose)

Two no scores at Misano in Italy despite a pre-race word from team boss Christian Sarron. (Gold & Goose)

the Belgarda Yamaha's team HQ in Italy. Edwards's team-mate for 1995 would be Yasutomo Nagai.

Nagai, or Yasu to his friends, was an experienced campaigner. At 29 years old, he'd been highly thought of by the Japanese factory for a few years. Back in 1994, he (along with a host of other Japanese wild-card riders) had impressed at his home round of Sugo, securing pole position and a best result of third in the opening race. In his past, he'd been considered good enough to partner Eddie Lawson at the 1994 Suzuka 8-Hour and had been sent to Europe to team up with the Sarron brothers, Dominique and Christian, the same year to help them win the Bol d'Or. He'd spent the past few seasons developing the YZF and the chance at full-time world glory was a thank you from Yamaha for all his hard work. Nagai was also on Yamaha Japan's payroll, not Belgarda's.

The 1995 season was important for Yamaha, as it was their big return to the WSB series in a factory capacity. In previous years Yamaha had supplied the likes of BYRD or Belgarda, which ran bikes that

featured factory parts, but this was the real McCoy. For 1995, the bikes were still effectively based at the Belgarda factory in Italy, but they were a world apart from any of the kitted machines. And so were the staff. No less a man than Christian Sarron – former 500cc GP winner – was the team manager, while Fiorenzo Fanali and Davide Brivio looked after the bikes. Fanalli had an impressive CV with Yamaha. He worked with Eddie Lawson during his title-winning years with the Japanese giant, before defecting with the Californian to the Cagiva 500 GP effort. During his time there he helped the blood-red machines to their debut win in 1992 in Hungary and through to 1993–94, where, in the hands of John Kocinski, the bikes became a title-threatening force.

The factory Yamaha YZF750SPs were different from the YZFs that Edwards had ridden for Vance & Hines in the US.

'No comparison, they were so different,' he says. 'The only thing that's the same between the 1995 bike and the 1993 and 1994 bikes I rode in the States is the

chassis. As far as the motor is concerned, Vance & Hines did the best they could with the parts they had, but that's not saying much. They didn't really have any special parts from the factory. The guys at Belgarda Yamaha had all the factory stuff, all the best parts and you really couldn't compare the AMA bike with the WSB bike.'

The YZF had already won a WSB race in the hands of diminutive hard-man Fabrizio Pirovano at Estoril, Portugal, on the BYRD machine in 1993, the bike's debut year. Since then Belgarda had run the likes of Mauro Lucchiari and Massimo Meregalli on their blue and yellow machines. With Mauro's defection to the all-conquering Ducati team, alongside Foggy, Paolo Casoli joined the Belgarda team for 1995. The two YZFs would be an interesting yardstick for the factory boys.

Hockenheim was the opening round. The track is basically a series of long, fast curves (curiously known as straights). It nestles in German woodland and a close

race is pretty much guaranteed thanks to the slipstreaming nature of the track. The Yamaha YZF750SP wasn't short on speed or ultimate horsepower, so it was expected that Colin and Nagai could do well.

Early on in race one, things were looking good. Colin was battling for third place with Troy Corser on his Promotor Ducati. Soon, Pierfrancesco Chili and Aaron Slight would pass the Texan, leaving him in a gaggle of riders chasing long-gone Fabrizio Pirovano and Fogarty in second and first respectively. At the flag, Edwards took a seventh place that could have been so much better had the Hockenheim slipstreaming lottery been as kind as it was to his team-mate Nagai, who netted a superb fourth. In race two, Edwards slipped into fifth place early on and held it to the flag, just behind Nagai who took another fourth.

Hockenheim was one of the few places that year where the YZFs ran the mid-range boosting EXUP valve. For years the device had given Yamaha's road bikes a useful kick of mid-range, which made them a bit more user-friendly. Normally such a gizmo would be junked immediately, sacrificed by the race tuner on the altar of ultimate power, especially as most four-cylinder race bikes spend their time in the final few thousands on the rev counter anyway.

'Yeah, we ran it at Hockenheim,' says Edwards, 'but not much after that race. In race bikes, I think the EXUP's like a theory that might be a good idea on paper, but in use it doesn't help much. You can't really feel a significant difference. We used it back in the States both years.'

While it was patently clear that the bike had enough power and speed, the harsh way in which it was delivered could pose a problem.

'The way the power came in sure was a problem on the YZF,' says Edwards. 'I think me and Yasu wanted a bike that would produce power from something like 8,000 revs and on, but with the YZF we only started making power from about 11,000. It kinda ran like a de-tuned old-style 'screamer'-motored 500 GP bike, but we had to live with it. Hockenheim went well as it was a top speed track and we were close to the others on top speed. But as soon as we got to tight tracks with lots of low-gear corners, we were in big trouble as we were really lacking in acceleration through the gears. That was the main problem. We needed a powerband that had more torque. I mean there was no torque, it was just horsepower at the end of the revs. There really was no powerband; it was just off or on. We could run it in that rev range so that it worked, but it was so narrow that to deliver it to the ground at any given time would just spin the rear.'

To back up Edwards's feelings for the bike, in 1996 the factory WSB machine would later find a home with the Cadbury's Boost Yamaha team in the British Superbike championship. Ex-500cc GP podium finisher Niall Mackenzie was looking forward to riding the bikes for that very reason.

Round two at Misano was a very different place to Hockenheim's peaky friendly long curves. Early on Edwards ran in the top ten, but then he ran wide on one of the many left-handers and was out of the points. Race two had a high-point. Edwards led his first

WSB race, albeit for a short time. Pretty soon he was swallowed up by the Ducatis of Lucchiari, Fogarty and Corser. Unsurprising, as this was Ducati's home track where the team did a lot of its testing. He eventually faded to seventh before retiring to the pits.

Round three was at Donington Park, a track that would later become an Edwards favourite. But in 1995 it was anything but. Nagai could only muster 14th in race one, improving to seventh in race two. Edwards's only points finish was a measly 12th in the second race.

One thing often forgotten when looking at the Yamaha team's results in the first half of the 1995 season was that their tyre suppliers, Dunlop, had suffered during the massive earthquake at their headquarters at Kobe in Japan. The results for Yamaha and Muzzy Kawasaki – the other factory running on Dunlops – would be better and more consistent towards the middle of the season.

'We had some big problems at the beginning of the year with the Dunlop tyres,' says Edwards, 'but they came a long way by the last part of the season. They produced a front that was just excellent, although at the time I thought the rear still needed a little bit of work. By Assen they were heading towards home plate instead of being on first base like they were at the start of the season. I guess the Kobe earthquake screwed up the whole development process and that's why it took some time to get the tyres good.'

With improved tyres after a few races came a change in the rules. With the Ducatis running away with things at the front, the ruling body, the FIM, announced a revision of the minimum weight limits. Since the debut WSB season in 1988, the original weight limits had stood at 140kg for twins and 165kg for four-cylinder bikes. In 1993 the twins were handed another 5kg on the minimum weight and then a year later the fours were given a shot in the arm when their minimum weight was reduced by a further 5kg, making the weight difference 15kg in the twins' favour. At the start of 1995, weight limits for both bike configurations were raised by 2kg to compensate for the lack of carbon disc brakes – now disallowed. Then the FIM decreed that the twins minimum weight would be raised 8kg to 155kg, while the fours were reduced

Things didn't get
any better at
Donington Park,
but at least
girlfriend Alyssia
was on hand to
hold the umbrella
and give some
support.
(Gold & Goose)

by 2kg to 160. It wouldn't make a great deal of difference, as Ducati could still make bigger holes in the
motor, from the then 926 and 955cc.

Monza, as always, produced some classic racing.
Similar to Hockenheim, it was a place where a peaky
race bike could score well. It proved to be the scene of
the team's and Edwards's first WSB podium. On the
first lap of race one, like many more experienced
Monza hands, he spent a lap or so hopping the
chicanes as he trod the fine line between hard braking
and outbraking. Early on, Edwards fought with
Piergiorgio Bontempi on the Bertocchi Kawasaki and
Simon Crafar on the Rumi Honda (which was effectively the second works Honda, following Doug Polen's
departure from the Castrol Honda squad). Meanwhile,
up front, Anthony Gobert on the Muzzy Kawasaki was
battling with Troy Corser's Promotor Ducati and Foggy.
Edwards finally got past Crafar, while up ahead, Corser
outbraked himself and tangled with Gobert. Both were
eaten up by one of Monza's ravenous gravel traps,
leaving Edwards in fourth. A further piece of good luck
for the Texan occurred near the end of the race, when

Chili lost the front of his Gattalone Ducati, to allow
Edwards through into third.

Race two provided another good team result, with
Nagai and Edwards battling it out together, while
Gobert and Foggy were entering the mesmerising
Parabolica corner side-by-side in the early stages.
Corser again crashed out. This time it wasn't his fault,
as he was bumped from behind by Bontempi's
Kawasaki. Chili went on to take his first WSB win,
while Nagai took fourth behind Slight and Fogarty.
Edwards was just behind his team-mate in fifth.

Albacete in Spain was the scene for round five of
the championship. Colin got a good start in race one
and lay in third place, before fading to tenth behind his
team-mate. Aaron Slight secured his first WSB win on
the RC45. Race two saw Edwards again behind his
team-mate at the flag, 11th this time to Nagai's sixth.

Any racer will tell you, the first person to beat is
your team-mate. If you're going to be judged against
anyone, it's your team-mate. Although Colin picked up
the first rostrum of the year for the factory debutantes,
he was consistently out-pointed by his team-mate,

which probably explains why Fogarty was telling him to beat his team-mate before criticising him.

Salzburgring was another low-point in the team-mate battle. Along the track's glorious curves, which again reward peaky, powerful bikes, Yasu had placed his bike on pole. Early in race one Colin was battling with the lesser YZF of Paolo Casoli and the Kawasaki of Bontempi, while Nagai was slipstreaming the likes of Slight on the RC45 and Corser on the Ducati. Eventually, Corser went wide on one of the final corners, but came back to take third behind a long-gone Gobert (second) with Foggy first. Slight came fourth ahead of Nagai, with Edwards back in ninth. Race two brought more bad luck for Edwards. This time, he was involved in a first-lap incident at the first chicane. Try as he might, Edwards couldn't avoid hitting the spinning body of Andreas Meklau, running over his head. He and Doug Polen (now on a privateer Ducati) took to the grass in an effort to avoid the Austrian. Later on in the race he retired, while Nagai was running in third and battling with Gobert, Bontempi, Slight and Pirovano. Corser eventually scored his maiden WSB win, with Nagai in fourth.

Laguna Seca – Edwards's home round. As at the Japanese and British rounds, the local talent came out to play in force. DuHamel and Mike Hale on the Smokin' Joe's Honda RC45s, and 'Fast' Freddie Spencer making one of his last outings on the Fast by Ferracci Ducati. Foggy's hatred of the track saw him down in 12th in qualifying, with the RC45 of Aaron Slight back in 18th. With his local knowledge and some of the WSB regulars so far behind on the grid, it was a good time to do well. Edwards led on the first lap, before battle was joined with Gobert and DuHamel on his AMA Honda. Eventually, Edwards was battling with Nagai and

Bounding around between Monza's glorious chicanes. A racetrack that would eventually see Colin's first and second win... (Gold & Goose)

Spencer, Fogarty having passed them all on a track he despises. Gobert eventually took his first 1995 win, ahead of Corser and DuHamel, with DuHamel's team-mate Mike Hale in fourth. Foggy came fifth ahead of Crafar's Honda, with Spencer next and Edwards just behind. Nagai came tenth. Race two saw the balance between Nagai and Edwards shift again as the Japanese rider netted fifth place and the American ninth, despite Colin being up front again in the early stages.

It was another example of Colin doing well earlier on, but then fading mid race.

Gobert's win capped a turnaround in his fortunes. As soon as Scott Russell defected to GPs, it was Gobert who got the attention his talent deserved. The WSB paddock said goodbye to Scott for a couple of years, while he chased his GP dream.

'Scott did what he knew he had to do,' says Edwards. 'You can't blame him at all. His biggest problem was that the Kawasaki was not competitive and he saw his career just going down the tubes. I think he should have gone to a 500 two years before that. For the three or four years prior, Scott Russell for me was the best Superbike rider in the world. Even when he was in the States, he was the best rider in the world. When WSB came over to Brainerd in 1991 Scott beat everyone except Polen, and that year Polen won nearly every race. At the time the rules were just so unfair.'

First time ever at Brands Hatch on a factory super-bike must rate as an interesting baptism of fire, especially if you consider what it must be like to take Paddock Hill Bend or Dingle Dell on a 160bhp machine. Edwards loved it: 'Brands is not a horsepower track, but a rider's track. You just put all the bumps and stuff out of your mind and just go.'

Race one saw Gobert, Fogarty and John Reynolds battle early on, with Nagai fourth, before Edwards began to get on terms with the leaders. In front of 45,000 home fans, Foggy had begun to make a break, leaving Gobert and Nagai to knock elbows and trade paintwork while Edwards made up places into fifth. He stayed there until the chequered flag came out on Fogarty's first ever Brands Hatch win.

Race two was better thanks to an improved start. Edwards was battling for second with Gobert, Reynolds,

Corser and Nagai. Fogarty was doing his familiar disap-pearing act, while Edwards duked it out with Gobert. It was a real edge-of-the-seat scrap, with Edwards going past Gobert into Paddock, only for the wild Aussie to ease off the brakes himself and go around the outside, a move not for the faint-hearted. Edwards then slipstreamed past the Kawasaki rider down the back straight into Hawthorns, only for Gobert again to best the Texan on the brakes. Later that lap, Edwards made a brave move past the green machine going into Dingle Dell. This time he made the pass stick and managed to pull away from Gobert. Behind this battle, Nagai was battling with Reynolds and they both closed on Gobert. Soon it became a three-way scrap for third, which Nagai won on the track. But the Japanese rider was deemed to have overtaken Reynolds under a yellow flag, which gave race control no option but to promote Reynolds into third place. Unfortunately for Reynolds,

...Also sees his first WSB podium in just the fourth round of his debut season. (Gold & Goose)

The team prepare the bike before Colin mounts his steed for another session. (Gold & Goose)

this came after the podium celebrations, so the rider from Nottingham didn't get to stand on the podium at his home round.

At round nine in Sugo, Nagai was on the front row, which was no surprise as the Japanese rider had impressed at his home round the year before. But, where Nagai was having no problems, Edwards was dogged by the YZF's punch out of corners.

'When we got to tracks where acceleration out of corners is important, just like Sugo in Japan, we had trouble,' says Edwards. 'Of course, Sugo was Nagai's home circuit and he knew it well so that helped him, but it went shit for me. Qualifying was good in the end as I took sixth place on the grid and I was pretty pleased with that. But the race was awful. The Hondas came out of the woodwork, they were everywhere, passing down the straightaway with maybe 5mph speed difference; it was disheartening.'

Extra Hondas in the shape of Takuma Aoki and Shinya Takeishi didn't help Edwards's chances of getting a good race finish, but neither did the better-

performing Kawasaki locals Keiichi Kitigawa and Katsuaki Fujiwara.

Nagai led race one for a few laps before Foggy made it past, only to suffer the mother of all highsides on the way out of a right-hander. You could count the seconds as Foggy's legs bicycled through the air before the agonising impact. The Briton staggered to his feet and limped to safety. The corner would later claim Takuma Aoki in similar circumstances. The race win went to Corser, with Castrol Honda's Slight in second and Nagai in third. Edwards was sixth.

Race two and, incredibly, Fogarty was on the grid just three hours after cracking two bones in his ankle and a small bone in his right hand, and badly bruising his hip. To make things even trickier, rain had fallen between the two races, but Foggy still went on to win, although Edwards's team-mate Nagai would prove to be the catalyst. Foggy was none too complimentary about Nagai's tactic of using his Ducati as a tow-truck to get a good time during practice in the 1995 season. Now, as they battled at the front, he was mad at being

'My dad dreamed up the helmet design. We did it before everyone else was using chequered flags on their helmets, but when they did Arai added the yellow flames. We designed it ourselves because we didn't fancy giving Troy Lee a big pay cheque! The replicas took three years to go on sale and they sold out in the US within a month.' (Gold & Goose)

Even on the shrieking banshee YZF, Colin's style was still smooth as silk. The 250 had taught him well. (Gold & Goose)

cut up twice by the local rider when he made his overtakes. Foggy was fuming and decided to show his displeasure once and for all by flicking him 'the bird' as he passed Nagai up the hill to the start-finish straight. Nagai eventually finished second, with Fujiwara third on the rapid home-grown Kawasaki. Colin was a distant tenth. By now Nagai was a superb fourth overall in the standings, behind Corser and Slight. No mean feat in his first year in world competition.

The legendary Circuit Van Drenthe at Assen played host to round ten. The British crowds and – it seemed – the British clouds turned up, as it rained on and off during qualifying.

Riding and racing in the wet is something that American riders have to get used to in Europe, as they don't do much of it at home. At Assen the rain was coming and going, which meant that the open circuit was drying in places. A wise head was needed for tyre choice, which is often critical at Assen. Edwards eventually out-qualified his team-mate. 'That wasn't saying much,' he recalls. 'I was running seventh before the track dried and I was bumped back to 11th. In the

wet I just put my head down and went for it. The traction available in the wet at Assen was unbelievable. It wasn't like anywhere else that year. Believe me, we rode in the rain in Misano during practice and it was a nightmare, unbelievable, but at Assen it was just fine. Qualifying could have been better, but it was bad timing really. We put a tyre on for the dry with five minutes to go and by the time I came round for a fast lap the chequered flag was out. So we got screwed in that sense, but that's the way it goes.'

But Edwards was enjoying the track in the wet, his smooth style helping him to a good time in the miserable conditions. 'I was getting along good with the track when it was wet. In the dry we had a real acceleration deficiency. We had loads of top speed but we were definitely lacking a little with respect to the other bikes, both two- and four-cylinders. It was one of the big problems we were trying to fix. The real key to fast times at Assen is being smooth, not trying to stuff it into every corner to be fastest from point A to B. You've got to link everything together in a smooth circuit and that's when you get a fast time.'

Whatever was happening to Edwards, Foggy had the title sewn up. Corser needed to win both races in Holland to postpone the inevitable till round 11 in Indonesia. But Carl is King of Assen and he toyed with Crafar on the works Honda before winning the race and the title by three seconds. Edwards's race was spent battling with Slight down in ninth place in the early laps before crashing out. Nagai was seventh. In race two Colin got a better start and was battling with Gobert, Fabrizio Pirovano and Reynolds for seventh. Late on in the race, disaster struck. Pirovano's Ducati retired with a terminal failure, which resulted in his factory 916 losing the contents of its sump on the fast Assen kinks. It was on this oil that Nagai crashed. In a cruel twist of fate, just as Yasu was sliding to a halt beside his machine, the bike seemed to dig into the ground, causing it to flip up

At home at Laguna saw a pair of points finishes. Here Colin takes on the notorious Corkscrew. (Gold & Goose)

Sharing the podium with Carl Fogarty in front of 45,000 fans. Things didn't get any bigger in WSB. (Gold & Goose)

in the air. The YZF landed on him causing massive head and chest injuries. Yasutomo Nagai was kept alive in intensive care until his family and girlfriend from Japan could attend his bedside and take the decision to switch off his life support. Within days the Yamaha WSB team made the decision to pull out of the remaining two races as a mark of respect. Yasu's death was the first in WSB's seven-year history.

'When Larry Schwarzbach died in 1992,' recalls Edwards, 'I cried like a baby. I was pretty upset. But that cured me, really. As bad as that seems, I'm going to qualify that and say that we're doing this because we want to and these are the risks we take. After Larry, when I heard about people going like that while racing, I thought, "Fuck, he died doing something he wanted to do and went out with a bang". It's tragic, I know, but I would rather go like that than be run over by a lorry. I did feel so very sorry for Nagai's girlfriend and parents. Dealing with it this way I think is the way racers grieve. You have to programme yourself to do it this way. Alyssia knows there's nothing she could do about it. You have to be a special kind of person to be a bike racer; you have to be a little bit different. Alyssia knows that it could happen.'

The decision to pull out of the final rounds wasn't something Colin wanted, although he respected the team's wishes. 'If they had told me to go, I would have gone. But it was done out of respect. It was their decision not to race – they didn't really ask me to, but I wanted to go.'

Yasu eventually dropped to fifth in the overall standings, behind Gobert, while Edwards was 11th, 44 points adrift. It had proved to be a real baptism of fire for Colin and the team.

At the end of 1995, Edwards said in an interview with Colin MacKellar: '1995 was basically one big test. The Ducati still stands head and shoulders above the others as far as off-corner acceleration is concerned, but the Honda has comparable grunt as well as decent top speed. It is a very fast motorcycle. Kawasaki has more or less the same problems as us, but they are faster. We need a new bike to build from and we'll definitely have a new bike in 1997, so I guess the new streetbike will be introduced in 1996.

My guess is it will have fuel injection, as we need something like that if we're serious about running for the world championship. The problem is that the bike is so old, there isn't much more we can do with it. The bike that Casoli was running via the Italian importer in 1994 is really the same bike as the one we are running. Maybe we could squeeze one more horsepower out of it, but the bike will become unreliable if we do much more to it.'

Looking forward to the coming years was something that Edwards had to do. He felt there was only so much that could be done with the YZF and he'd heard that there was a new machine on the horizon. As it turned out, the new bike would not turn up until 1999, two years later than he originally thought (although a road bike, the YZF-R1 did show up at that time and was tested by Edwards). One thing he did have on his side was his age. He was still only 21 and his contract with Yamaha wouldn't run out until the end of 1997. The company had a plan for him, just like they did way back when he was in youth motocross when he was a works rider at the age of 12. But was his future with WSB or GPs? He was young enough to risk in GPs and still have years to work at it and come good.

In an interview at the time, he said: 'GPs is definitely where I want to go. It's hard to think of four years from now when you want to win this year or next year. Sure, if I stay with Yamaha I could probably go to GPs and in four or five years time learn how to ride the thing and get it developed and maybe win a championship. But I'm concentrating on the immediate future.'

The obvious route for Edwards was with Yamaha and Team Roberts. 'I'd talked with them about my ambitions and what they were going to be doing and I think we had the same view, but it was a question of when.'

With 500 deity Mick Doohan on the Roberts shopping list for 1996, it was no surprise that Edwards was going to stay in the WSB fold for the foreseeable future. After all, for 1996 Roberts had a young star in Norick Abe – that meant a young star that was agreeable with the Japanese at the factory – and a few other hot properties in the shape of Kenny Roberts Junior,

Assen. Colin was doing well in the wet during practice, but lost out in qualifying when the conditions improved. The weekend would end on a very sad note for the team. (Gold & Goose)

Loris Capirossi and Jean-Michel Bayle. Again, in an interview at the time, he realised his time would come. 'I could spend another two years with these guys to see out the three-year WSB deal with Yamaha and I'll still only be 23. You've got to swallow your ego, swallow your pride and bide your time. Be patient. Your turn will come.'

Another reason why things weren't happening for Edwards was that his father was the one who normally handled the management role, but he was sidelined for a while during 1995. 'Dad was looking after some of this stuff for me, but he had a liver transplant so he was out of things. Everything went perfectly. They stuck it in, it worked fine,' says Edwards.

His dad remembers one conversation with his son just after the operation: 'Colin did a little bit of work with a manager while I was having the operation. Then just after I had the transplant, Colin rang me. He said: "Dad, you okay? Are you going to live?" I said I was fine, then he replied. "Good, 'cause this manager guy wants too much money." I looked after Colin's interests for another few years until I had a spinal problem. Since then Colin's looked after his own interests.'

All in all, 1995 had been a tough year. 'I guess I struggled at some circuits, but no one said it was going to be easy.'

One thing he said to Colin MacKellar at the time is worthy of note. 'I'd like to see Fogarty get on a four-cylinder bike and have to work for a living. Then he'd find out just how fast these guys on four-cylinder bikes really are. He'd be stupid to do it. You know you're on the best bike so use it. He knows if he gets off that bike then Corser's just going to win if he keeps the thing together.'

Colin tried to make an appearance at his home round in 1997, but even with an external cast, it was too painful and the risks were too great. (Gold & Goose)

ridin' the
whale

Early in 1996 Edwards was looking forward to the new World Superbike season, but again he was not too enamoured with riding the YZF750SP. Compared with other machines in the series, it was felt that the YZF was a little long in the tooth, even if it was blisteringly fast.

'I'm not going to bullshit,' says Edwards, 'but in 1995 the bike was kinda like a wild animal. I felt that once we had it tamed we could win races. I had to learn to ride all over again during that year. It would spin the rear wheel out of every corner. Second gear acceleration was excellent, but it was all a bit too instant, and never very smooth.'

This was something that weighed heavily on the minds of Belgarda Yamaha technicians like Fiorenzo Fanali. 'The power delivery at the top of the rev range is simply a characteristic of the Yamaha,' he said at the time. 'We do not need any more power, just more torque.' The team had worked hard with Öhlins – the Yamaha-owned suspension subsidiary from Sweden – to get the power to the ground more effectively. A new suspension linkage midway through the 1995 season went some way to helping, but the real problem was one of engine configuration and capacity. The 955cc Ducatis simply had the ability, thanks to the way the twin makes its power and the size of the holes in the engine, to pull away out of the corners. 'They have a power and a torque advantage,' shrugged Fanali. 'At Misano in 1995 we struggled for grip while Ducati just fitted a long first gear and pulled out of corners no problem. That would be impossible with the YZF, as there's nothing happening at 3,000rpm.' Yamaha race

engineer Takaaki Suzuki also felt that Edwards's history on the 250 stroker was a problem. 'He was riding it like a two-stroke, as if he was searching for a powerband.' Bizarre, especially as before 1995 Colin had been riding a four-stroke for much of his career.

Still, for 1996 the real deal for the Milan-based Belgarda squad was making sure that the impressive power output got to the ground more effectively. Chassis development was going to be paramount for 1996 and to this end the Belgarda team brought Öhlins man Anders Andersson into the team. Andersson was *the* man in suspension in the WSB paddock. Alongside Foggy's chief mechanic Anthony 'Slick' Bass, Andersson was one of the men that many paddock watchers said was a major force in Foggy's dominant 1995 campaign. Andersson and the team simply had to make the YZF that bit more user-friendly.

The structure at the top of the team also changed, with Christian Sarron departing the team manager's slot and handing the reins to Davide Brivio.

Edwards's wish to see Foggy on a four-cylinder bike was to be answered, as just before the end of the 1995 season Carl had decided to make the switch from the all-conquering Virginio Ferrari-run Ducati Corse squad to Castrol Honda. At the international season opener at Daytona in March, a veritable phalanx of WSB and GP stars were on hand to blow away the cobwebs before the main assault on the season began. Edwards was going for his first superbike win at Daytona, along-side fellow WSB regulars Troy Corser and Mike Hale on their Promotor Ducatis and Anthony Gobert on his

A third of the way through his contract with Yamaha USA in World Superbike, Colin was back on the 'Whale', as he called his three-year-old YZF. (Gold & Goose)

Colin leads Pierfrancesco Chili's Ducati at Donington Park. (Gold & Goose)

Muzzy Kawasaki. Making a special appearance on the all-new Suzuki GSX-R750 was returning 500cc GP star Scott Russell, who was aiming for his fourth Daytona 200 race victory aided and abetted by his Lucky Strike Suzuki squad. During practice it was Corser who set the pace, prompting Russell to echo Edwards's, Slight's and his own earlier words that the rules just weren't fair. 'The Ducati should be in GPs,' he said at the time. 'Foggy on the four-cylinder this year, he won't win a race, let alone the championship.'

In a rain-postponed Daytona, Russell came off second best to the Honda of DuHamel, although only just. Edwards was a superb third.

In early testing for the 1996 season, I met Edwards for the first time. As a reporter for *Motor Cycle News*, I was mindful of the previous year's clashes in the newspaper between Edwards and Foggy. I was introduced as Chris Herring's replacement at *MCN*. 'Chris Herring's replacement? Great, whoopee do! That's just

great.' It was clear that Edwards wasn't too enamoured with *MCN*'s ex-WSB reporter, who had taken over PR for the Castrol Honda team after playing a key role in firing-up stories for the world's biggest biking newspaper. Ironically, a friendship between the two would develop when Colin moved to Castrol Honda in 1998, the pair both sharing a passion for golf.

On 14 April the first round of the 1996 WSB championship kicked off in Ducati's backyard, Misano. John Kocinski, drafted in to replace Fogarty, was untouchable all weekend, with pole position and two wins, albeit only after race two 'winner' Gobert was ruled out on a techincal infringement. Edwards was a disappointing 11th and seventh after experiencing tyre and suspension problems all weekend. He was behind Fogarty in both races, even though the Briton was having a 'nightmare' opening round. Colin's team-mate Wataru Yoshikawa – another Japanese favourite son in the tradition of the late Nagai – was ahead of

Colin in race one, but behind him in the second. Donington Park saw some improvement for Edwards and the other four-cylinder riders on the flowing circuit. Colin took part in a massive battle for second place in race one, although he faded to sixth. Better was to come in race two, with a fighting fourth place. In both races he finished ahead of Fogarty.

Hockenheim was a turning point for Fogarty and his standing in the eyes of the other four-cylinder riders. After a string of bad results and the sacking of his mechanic Slick Bass, Fogarty was at an all-time low. To make matters worse, the opening race was won by his team-mate Slight, while Colin slipstreamed his way to third. Race two was a classic. Fogarty had altered the rear ride height on his RC45 and managed to hang with the leading group in the second race, outbraking Slight into the stadium to take his first win on the four-cylinder machine. In the press conference afterwards came a quote from Foggy that was made for those who had doubted him. 'People said I couldn't win races on the Honda. Now I see them crawling under stones.' After that first RC45 win, Scott Russell phoned Carl to offer his congratulations.

Monza again. Similar to Hockenheim, where the power and grunt of the Honda should do the trick and also where the Yamaha's top end should place Edwards and Yoshikawa near the top. Once more the Hondas were in striking distance of the twins and the legendary track produced some very close racing. Fogarty won the first race from Slight with Edwards third. In the second encounter, Chili took a home win on a Ducati, with Slight second and Foggy third. This time Edwards could only manage fifth, but the slipstreaming, outbraking lottery of Monza meant that fifth could so easily have been a podium.

After Monza an incredible thing happened. Most racers will never admit they've been wrong. The fragile racing psyche can't really handle it; you have to maintain an edge. But Edwards is different, he's an honest guy, 'just plain old Colin from Texas' as he likes to describe himself. So when Fogarty had proved his skill on the four-cylinder Honda, Edwards had to do what he had to do. He knocked on Fogarty's motorhome after the race, where Carl's family were helping him celebrate his win, and said in front of them all that he was wrong to criticise him. As Edwards said afterwards: 'Man, after Carl

kicked my ass at Monza, I had to shake him by the hand.' It was the beginning of mutual respect between the two, if not mutual friendship.

At Monza Edwards had a new part-time team-mate, Jamie Whitham. The rider from Huddersfield was doing well in the *MCN*-backed British Superbike championship on his Cadbury's Boost Yamaha (using Colin's 1995 bikes) and got the chance to fill in for an injured Wataru Yoshikawa. Edwards had the measure of the Briton, who managed an impressive seventh and sixth.

Whitham was – and still is – a close friend of Carl Fogarty, and now he was teamed up with the young American who had clashed in the 1995 war of words with his friend.

'I just told him straight,' says Whit. 'I said Carl is my best mate, so I don't want to hear anything daft, but to be honest he was sound and we got on fine.'

Edwards and Whitham soon struck up a friendship that carried on through Jamie's 1997 and 1998 seasons in WSB with Suzuki and still exists today.

'Jamie's great,' says Edwards. 'His wife Andrea and Alyssia were both pregnant at the same time and Andrea had Ruby only a short while before we had

Gracie. He rang me up and said [adopts deep, northern English sounding voice] "Aye oop, Colin, we've had a baby".'

The Czech Republic played host to the next round. While the Hondas made the running for the four-cylinder machines, again taking the fight to Ducati, Edwards was left to pick up a sixth and seventh as he battled with tyre problems. One thing that was reversed from 1995 was that he was most definitely getting the better of fancied Japanese team-mate Yoshikawa, who was battling back from injury. Edwards's home race at Laguna Seca should have been better, but a fourth in race one behind Kocinski, Corser and Britain's Neil Hodgson (celebrating his first podium in WSB) was not bettered as Edwards crashed at the infamous Corkscrew on the first lap of race two. It was the halfway point in the season and Edwards was lying in fifth place overall, behind Kocinski, and 81 points behind leader Corser. Yoshikawa shone at the event for two reasons. First, he took the YZF to a lap record around the Californian circuit. Then, during a press conference (albeit after much silent debate with Aaron Slight), the Japanese rider told the assembled journalists

Into Goddards hairpin at Donington. (Gold & Goose)

Edwards's 1996 team-mate was another of Yamaha's favourite sons – Wataru Yoshikawa. (Gold & Goose)

Fanali and Edwards were joined by suspension ace Anders Andersson from Öhlins in the Yamaha team. (Gold & Goose)

that he would: 'Kick ass!' Would you get that sort of press conference in GPs?

Perhaps the high-point of the season came next, a Suzuka 8-Hour win, Colin's first. The RC45s were favourites for the race, with Slight winning the last two outings on the V4. Slight and 500cc GP team-mate Tadayuki Okada made the early running, with Okada taking an early lead and handing over to Slight. Then, exiting turn two, Slight crashed and broke two of his toes. Despite this, he rode back to the pits, where the prognosis on the injury meant the two favourites had to retire. After the crash, Fogarty and Takuma Aoki were promoted to first place before disaster struck Honda again, with Foggy eating gravel, although this time the damage was repairable. The second Honda crash promoted the YZF of Edwards and 21-year-old Noriyuki Haga, a tough All-Japan competitor, into first position. Despite there being five teams on the lead lap, the duo kept up the pressure to win ahead of Gobert and Crafar's Kawasaki. Fogarty and Aoki salvaged third.

Edwards and Haga were the toast of Japan – it's not for nothing that the Japanese rate the 8-Hour as a bread-and-butter race for their aspiring factory stars. Gifts were heaped upon the winners, with Yamaha

giving generous bonus gifts for the win at Honda's home circuit. Edwards chose a Yamaha grand piano for his home in Texas.

'I did want to ask for a car, but as Yamaha don't build them I guessed the piano would be a neat gift.'

Back to WSB and Brands Hatch, a circuit quickly becoming a firm favourite with Edwards. In front of 60,000 British bike fans, Chili took the first race win ahead of Gobert and Kocinski; Edwards was a fine fourth. Better was to come in race two, when Edwards took his third podium of the year after battling hard with Gobert's Kawasaki for third place.

Sentul, Indonesia, saw more good points finishes for Edwards, with fifth and fourth places. Consistency was keeping Colin in fifth place overall, not too far behind the championship battling quartet of Corser, Slight, Fogarty and Kocinski. Impressively, Edwards was ahead of Chili, a race winner at Brands Hatch, in the overall points table.

Round nine and it was the same old story at Sugo as myriad Japanese works machines crawled out of the woodwork to take on the WSB regulars. Both races were won by RC45s, but not in the hands of the Castrol Honda riders Slight and Fogarty. Instead, Japanese stars Yuichi Takeda and Takuma Aoki took a win apiece, the first double for the RC45. Things weren't so good for Edwards. A crash in practice put him out of the proceedings for a couple of weeks with a broken collarbone. In race one his team-mate Yoshikawa was duking it out with All-Japan star and Edwards's 8-Hour team-mate Haga on the yellow number 57 YZF. Pretty soon Yoshikawa was dropped, as was Corser's Ducati (Haga's pass around the outside of the Australian going into the final chicane was a portent for the future), leaving Haga to race it out to the finish with Takeda on the HRC bike. On the last lap, Haga entered and exited the chicane in the lead, heading towards what was expected to be Yamaha's and the YZF's first win since Estoril in Portugal in 1993 in the hands of Fabrizio Pirovano. But the tortuous climb up Sugo's start/finish straight saw the low-down punch of the RC45 out-drag the peaky YZF – the pair clashed fairings over the line, with the V4 just ahead. Yoshikawa was third, disappointed at being beaten by Haga despite being the official rider in the WSB team. 'I am not happy. I should be the first Yamaha at Sugo,' he said. What Edwards could have done against the Honda and Haga was a matter for debate.

Race two and Haga crashed out. The Yamaha challenge faded, although Norihiko Fujiwara netted fifth ahead of a frustrated Yoshikawa in eighth.

Edwards sat out Assen, where his place was taken by super-sub Jamie Whitham. Whit took sixth in the opening race, before taking to the grass in race two and eventually salvaging 14th. Meanwhile, Fogarty took a memorable double – the first same-person double – on the RC45.

With a month off before the next round in Albacete, Spain, Edwards had time to make a full recovery from his collarbone injury. He qualified on the front row in third place, ahead of Fogarty and behind Kocinski in second and pole-sitter Corser. Edwards battled with the leaders throughout the race, passing Fogarty's RC45 and then catching and passing Kocinski's Ducati for third place. Up ahead was Chili and, further up the road, Corser. With Edwards putting more pressure on the Italian, Chili succumbed and crashed, leaving Edwards second – his best result of the year so far, although he and the other Dunlop runners were particularly strong towards the end of the race. In the second race he again mugged some impressive scalps, taking both Fogarty and Edwards to claim third place behind Corser and Kocinski.

The final race of the season at Phillip Island was a sort of half-home round for Edwards. Back in the saddle at his home round was Anthony Gobert, who had returned after missing a few rounds due to injury. At the time many thought he'd simply gone AWOL, while he counted down time towards his done-deal

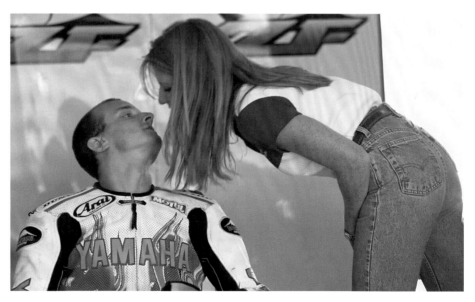

Alyssia was looking after her man again in 1996. (Gold & Goose)

with the Lucky Strike Suzuki GP squad. Colin secured pole position, the second of his WSB career. He went into the first turn in second place, before taking the lead, a lead he would almost hold to the flag. It was Edwards as we would come to know him in the future, smooth, unruffled and in control, right up until the moment Gobert slid up the inside going into one of Phillip Island's slower corners. So near, yet so far, Gobert held on until the flag. It had been Edwards's most impressive showing yet.

The second heat and Colin was again up at the front, although coming into the first corner Corser hit one of Phillip Island's many resident seagulls and sent the remains spinning into Edwards's radiator. At the end of the first lap it was Edwards's turn to make close acquaintance with a feathered friend. This time one hit his YZF full on, smashing his screen and blurring the visor on his Arai lid with blood. Despite this he held on to third. At the end of the season, Corser took the title

ahead of Slight, Kocinski and Fogarty. Edwards was way out of touch of the top four, but had pulled away from Chili and taken fifth overall in the standings thanks to some consistent rides.

In summing up 1996, it has to be said that 1997 promised so much. Despite being a little long in the tooth – although only a year older than the Honda – the YZF was maturing well. Towards the end of the 1996 season Edwards's two pole positions and four rostrums suggested even better for 1997, and almost reflected his coming of age in the AMA series back in 1994. After two seasons with two of Japan's 'favourite sons' as team-mates, 1997 signified a new dawn for Yamaha when the company signed 1993 WSB champion Scott Russell from 500cc GPs. Edwards had admired Russell for many years and Scott was happy to be back in the superbike paddock, which looked on him as a favourite son. 'When the Suzuki GP thing was going bad, I was looking at coming back into WSB. Kel

Brands brought
another podium...
(Gold & Goose)

...While Japan
brought two
no scores.
(Gold & Goose)

COLIN EDWARDS RIDIN' THE WHALE

Edge [respected WSB snapper and journalist/author] mentioned Yamaha as they have such a good family atmosphere,' said Russell at the time.

Indeed they did. The Belgarda Yamaha team in its two seasons had taken to the more relaxed WSB paddock well. Even if the team had yet to win a race, it was an established set up. Team boss Davide Brivio boasted that in two seasons only one mechanic had left. 'We've not changed anyone else, apart from the riders. Not the cook, no one in hospitality. That is very good for our team.' It was little wonder, as the cook was excellent. Perhaps Davide had forgotten Christian Sarron's departure at the end of 1995, but on the whole he was right. It was the friendliest set up in the paddock and one that Russell was looking forward to joining after the trials and tribulations of the Lucky Strike Suzuki squad in 500cc GPs. Journalists also warmed to the Belgarda team. Chatting to Brivio was always easier than trying to get quotes out of the slightly caustic Rob Muzzy of Muzzy Kawasaki or tight-lipped Neil Tuxworth of Castrol Honda.

Edwards was also looking forward to working with Scott. 'Since Scott's joined…,' he said at the time, 'we've become a real team. It was a little bit tough with two Japanese riders – Yasu and Wataru – because they hardly spoke any English. They spoke Japanese to Japanese engineers and… broken English to me. So I didn't really feel the communication there was really spot on. Now that Scott's here, we can do so much in a day's worth of testing; two or three times as much as we did before, simply because we communicate so well.'

Yamaha obviously thought the pairing of Edwards and Russell would bear fruit for the Japanese factory. In fact, the company laid on a lavish team launch in Italy at the end of 1996 and the assembled journalists were given a Russell or Edwards signed Shoei or Arai replica lid, just so that they 'would know who to look out for in 1997'.

79

Australia was
a high point on
which to end
1996 with pole
position, a second
in race one...
(Gold & Goose)

...and a third
in race two.
(Gold & Goose)

Australia 1997:
new team-mates
Colin and Scott
Russell take some
time out on a
brace of Yamaha
RoadStars.
(Gold & Goose)

Away from the glitz of the launch the work began for the 1997 season at Daytona. Russell went to the 200-mile event looking for his fourth win (he'd won three times on a Kawasaki and just missed out in 1996 on the Suzuki), while Edwards was looking for that first elusive 200 win. No one saw which way Scott went in the race. Doug Chandler, who would eventually take his third AMA Superbike title later that year, came second. Third was Edwards. Podiums at Daytona were becoming a frustratingly frequent event for the Texan, as were podiums in WSB.

So often the bridesmaid, Edwards knew he had to make that physically small, but psychologically immense step from second or third on the podium to first. Despite this, and the solid work of the previous two seasons, 1997 – his final contracted year with Yamaha – promised much, but ultimately failed to deliver.

Disappointingly for Edwards at least, the 'whale' still looked and felt the same, even if there had been changes under the skin.

Mid-range torque had been the holy grail at the Belgarda team for the past few seasons. A modified intake and lighter cranks made the venerable inline four spin up easier, boosting power in the 8,000 to 10,000rpm range, just where Edwards's 1995 machine had been lacking. But, for 1997, the team was looking at wringing just that little bit more top-end power as well to tackle the likes of Ducati and Honda. 'In Japan our engineers have tried to give the bike more torque and then we concentrated on top-end power,' Brivio revealed. 'For 1997 the riders were happy with the level of torque the engines produced. Our acceleration wasn't so bad, so maybe we had forgotten to look at top-end power a little as we went for more torque. It's

difficult working with an engine that has been around for so many years as our engineers had done pretty much all they could with it. Despite all this our engine was very competitive.'

Elsewhere there were further improvements. The YZF's swing-arm was the subject of a minor change, while Yamaha's continued close relationship with daughter-company Öhlins, saw the introduction of improved rear suspension and front forks.

With the WSB season starting back in Australia, Edwards's superb performances at Phillip Island in 1996 were still fresh in people's memories.

The track's notoriously unpredictable weather made for an interesting first race of the season. Edwards was one of many to crash out of the first race, leaving Kocinski (who had swapped positions over the winter with Fogarty, between Ducati and Castrol Honda) to win ahead of the Briton; Kawasaki's Simon Crafar came third. Race two was a re-run of Edwards's 1996 so-near-yet-so-far race at 'the Island', but crueller. Edwards spent the race battling with Crafar and Slight, and it was obvious the winner would come from these three. Crafar and Edwards were both looking for a debut win, while Slight was looking to convert his pole position into his first win of the year. The final few corners were classic. Edwards was ahead and had opened up a gap on the Kiwi. Many think he was finally going to get his due, a maiden WSB win. But Slight was too clever to let that happen. He used all his skill on the brakes to get just close enough on the long final left hander to sling-shot past the Texan just as they got to the line.

It was almost too cruel for words. But it was also just racing. 'I just managed to get Colin back under braking at Honda corner, despite the gap he'd pulled out. Then I just had to stay with him around the final corner and down the straight,' said Slight.

Simple, if you have a Honda. Despite coming so close, Edwards was ever his reflective self.

'Well, I guess Phillip Island is the closest I came to winning on the old YZF!' he says. 'I came out of the last turn and the Honda had the punch out of the corner and Aaron beat me. That's just racing; that's what happens.'

At Misano and round two of the series, Edwards's team-mate Russell – perhaps echoing his previous team troubles in GPs – turned up a day late after being caught speeding in his Porsche Turbo back home in the States. By the time he and the Belgarda team got out on the track it was apparent that rain was becoming the predominant feature of the year. For the two Yamaha teamsters it would be a bizarre race. Russell was to be one of main men in the wet, trading places with 1997's rain-man, Kocinski. Eventually, and strangely, both Russell and Kocinski lapped Edwards. Then, soon after Russell crashed, Edwards was classified sixth overall. Race two was again wetter than an otter's pocket. Scott again shot away in the torrential conditions, but Chili soon went after him before he slowed with a mechanical problem. Russell, on his spare bike, began to go backwards, he eventually finished sixth, two places ahead of his Texan team-mate.

Round three was at Donington, and it was here that Neil Hodgson snatched the first pole position of his WSB career. Edwards and Russell battled it out for fifth and sixth in race one, the younger man just getting the nod over the 1993 WSB champ. Both

finished ahead of wild-card British Superbike champ Niall Mackenzie on the year-old factory YZF. Race two was a repeat for the two Belgarda team-mates, although one place further down in sixth and seventh. It wasn't turning out the way 1996 and round one at Phillip Island had suggested. At Hockenheim, and round four, history was on the YZF's side. Rev-happy four-cylinder engines like the Yamahas were rewarded with results. Kawasaki and Crafar – who, along with team-mate Yanagawa, was revelling in a new engine with better top-end performance – took pole, the first of his career. Despite the new hardware, Crafar's motor broke chasing Slight, which left Kocinski to snatch second ahead of Russell. Russell's was a lonely four-cylinder fight against a horde of twins, battling with his old nemesis Fogarty, as well as Hodgson and Chili. When Slight took his chance in the last right hander going into the stadium to pass Kocinski for the lead, so did Russell, giving him his first podium as a Yamaha WSB rider. Edwards was back down in seventh place. Race two saw Edwards take fifth behind Russell – the portents weren't good. After comprehensively beating his 1996 team-mate, Colin was in danger of being overshadowed by his illustrious 1997 team-mate. After four rounds, Edwards was in fifth overall, just two points ahead of the man from Georgia.

Monza, and round five, was effectively the Belgarda Yamaha team's home race. With the team workshops located just minutes away from the legendary circuit it was useful as a test track for the team. In fact, with a long and successful test scheduled just prior to the race, pole position and a win looked a distinct possibility. Turning up at the races on electric-blue Yamaha France YZFs were Jean-Philipe Ruggia and Jean-Marc Deletang. Ruggia was to ruin Edwards's 1997 season completely, when he knocked him off in free practice on the Saturday morning. Edwards fractured his wrist then found out a few weeks later that he'd broken the plate that had held his collarbone together since Sugo in 1996. Ruggia said of the incident: 'This was racing.' Funny that everyone else was convinced it was practice. Russell's pole position later that day did little to lift the team's spirits.

Edwards missed his home round at Laguna. Before he went to Brands, he travelled to the 8-Hour to try to replicate his 1996 win, again teamed with Noriyuki

The calm before the race day storm. Good weather for practice preceded a downpour on race day at Misano in 1997. (Gold & Goose)

Lining up for Donington Park practice with Neil Hodgson (foreground) and James Haydon (background). (Gold & Goose)

Haga, but without success. It was then that he realised his injury was too serious for him to compete. Eventually he discovered that his injuries from Monza would require further surgery and a few more weeks' convalescence. His place in the squad for European rounds was taken over by Chris Walker, who was doing well in the British Superbike series on the Cadbury's Boost Yamaha.

The 1997 season would eventually prove to be John Kocinski's year. The American from Little Rock, Arkansas (although more a Californian after years of living there), overcame the RC45's problems – although only after the team overcame his problems. Both eventually worked together to take the title in Sugo, Japan. Russell soldiered on, regularly beating part-time team-mate Walker and getting a best result of second at Brands Hatch. The embarrassment for both regular teamsters was the emergence of new star Noriyuki Haga. The newly-crowned All-Japan champion took second behind Akira Yanagawa's Kawasaki in race one and succeeded where Russell and Edwards had failed, taking the YZF to it's first win since 1993 in the second race. The Japanese star's immediate impact on WSB was apparent.

Leading Simon
Crafar's Kawasaki
in the race at the
Esses. The Kiwi
would beat Colin
in both heats.
(Gold & Goose)

Old pals' act.
Colin gives Jamie
Whitham a lift
back to the pits
at Hockenheim.
(Gold & Goose)

As if to rub it in, Nori-Chan appeared in the final race of the year at Sentul and took fifth and third, ahead of Russell in sixth and fifth.

The year drew to a close under a black cloud for Edwards, one that had chased him since Monza.

'Yeah, being taken out by Ruggia wasn't fun,' he recalls. 'Thanks to that incident I was out all year, which took me to the end of my final contracted year. I was worried I would be out of a job, I mean, I was freakin' out. I thought "that is that". I was thinking that I'd have to go ride AMA again.'

Did Haga's impressive performance make him better than all the regular riders that had gone before? What made him and the YZF click, where it never had with the combined talents of Edwards, Russell, Nagai and Yoshikawa – or super-subs like Whitham, Walker and local wild cards like Mackenzie?

'The YZF was never a world-beater,' says Colin. 'It would work well at some tracks and never at others. It was just never consistent enough and that's what wins world titles.'

Either way, it was clear that Yamaha in Japan would prefer to use Haga-san's services for 1998, as he'd delivered when everyone else hadn't. Conveniently, this was the end of Colin's three-year deal with the Yamaha factory. He wasn't too downhearted, as he thought there was an opening in 500cc GPs with Yamaha.

'I had three great years racing with Yamaha in WSB, met a lot of good people and had a lot of fun,' he says. 'For 1998, I was supposed to go ride in the Red Bull Yamaha team alongside Simon Crafar. I was

keen on it, so my dad and Peter Clifford started talking. It turned out that I was going to take a third cut in my salary to go GP racing with Red Bull Yamaha. Well, I don't really know what happened there, maybe my dad was hard to bargain with, but the next thing I know, Regis Laconi has the ride. I'm thinking, "Fuck! I've got nothin'!"'

Fortunately, something else came up. 'So at the end of 1997 my dad rang Neil Tuxworth. At the time John Kocinski had just won the title for Castrol Honda and, as part of his deal, he was going to race with Sito Pons' team in 500s. He told my dad that he had no idea that I was available, so we all decided to do it.'

Time clouds things, but Castrol Honda team boss Tuxworth remembers it a little differently.

A pile of tattered bodywork indicated the end of Colin's season. (Gold & Goose)

'We rang Colin up and there was a good reason for it. I always rated Colin, even before he rode for us. At the time we'd just lost John Kocinski and Castrol was a bit upset about that as they wanted a US rider for the market out there. I spoke to Colin at the end of 1997 and he was at a low ebb after sitting out the major part of the 1997 season. We talked about it for a while and made the deal. At first Honda wasn't interested in a rider that was contracted to another Japanese factory, as they thought Colin was still linked with Yamaha; also they felt he was known too much as 'Yamaha's' rider. The thing was, he wasn't contracted to them and now he's more known as a Honda rider – even after the Aprilia deal.'

Whatever, Edwards was going to be racing the awesome and fickle RC45 in 1998.

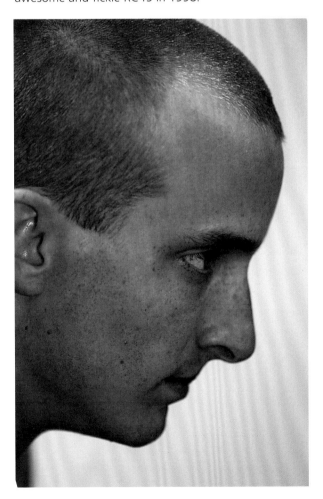

Considering his options at the end of 1997 and the end of his Yamaha contract. (Gold & Goose)

A study in
concentration.
(Graeme Brown)

title
challenger

Edwards and Castrol Honda PR man Chris Herring had never seen eye-to-eye. He saw Chris as the main perpetrator behind the fantastical 'Colin the cockroach' stories in *Motor Cycle News* back in 1995. But that was back when Chris, or 'Kipper' as he's known to many in the worldwide race paddock, was a newspaper hack for *MCN*. Chris, ever a lover of motorcycle racing, always wanted to get his beloved sport in the pages of *MCN* and – better still – the daily nationals. The single-minded way in which he chased a story even left hardened racers quivering in their boots, and their motorhomes.

'Sometimes when Chris Herring knocked on my door, I'd pretend I was out,' said Simon Crafar in 1996, following the combative journalist's move into PR. Any rebuff to his stories in *MCN* would be met with a Northallerton accented rebuff: "What are yer saying,

man? You've got some bloody coverage; you're in the paper".' As a journalist, Chris fully believed that racers were human like the rest of us and that their elevated status meant that you could – and probably should – make life for them as uncomfortable as possible in the bid to get a good story.

Things changed for Chris. From 1996 he became Castrol Honda's PR man, before evolving into myriad other roles, including sponsorship man, marketing man and general fix-it bloke. Think James Garner's role as 'Blagger' in *The Great Escape* and you won't be far wrong. If you wanted something, chances were Kipper could sort it. Bizarrely, Chris and Colin were now working together and both had learned to respect each other's roles in the Castrol Honda team.

'It was really strange,' recalls Chris. 'During an early

Esconced in his new team in Australia. Colin with new crew chief Adrian Gorst standing behind him alongside team boss Neil Tuxworth. (Gold & Goose)

1998 test Colin was getting changed in the articulated transporter/office, which comes to every test and WSB round, while I was working. Halfway through he stopped, turned to me and said, "Dude, I never thought we'd be working together like this".' Despite their testy beginnings in 1995, both would become firm friends.

With the Castrol Honda team in general and the fickle RC45, Colin was also making serious in-roads.

During the 1997 season, John Kocinski, who appeared to have an on-off switch in place of a talent gland, made the grade. He became the first rider to take a GP and WSB title in a year dominated by poor weather. All this heaped more pressure on Aaron Slight. The Kiwi had suffered through Kocinski's weird habits, team-mate psyche-outs and the Castrol Honda team's strange acceptance and accommodation of his destructive persona. Slight welcomed a team-mate who he got on with and respected. It was the first time this had happened since Doug Polen two years earlier.

According to Slight's excellent autobiography, *You Don't Know The Half Of It*, Aaron went into 1998 with a change of philosophy. He felt he needed a change of background and team set-up. He moved to Monaco and switched from long-time chief mechanic Adrian Gorst to Norris Farrow. Slight also had ideas as to who he wanted his team-mate to be. In his book he says: 'I was keen to see Scott Russell signed. Honda evidently didn't like Scott's attitude, so they signed his Yamaha team-mate Colin Edwards instead. He had been due to switch over from superbikes to 500s that year but he held out for too much money and was frozen out of a ride. I rang Colin and suggested he gave Honda a call. Honda picked him up on the rebound and, after Kocinski, Colin seemed pleasant and easy going for an American.'

The Kiwi and the RC45 had to be favourite for 1998. Aaron had been training harder than ever for his campaign, while the RC45 had also been improved for its fifth season.

The biggest change of all to the bike was a visual one. Gone was the old single-sided swing-arm, which, anyway, was more of a marketing ploy than a performance aid. In came a traditional double-forked item, which, while 1kg (2.2lb) heavier than the single-sider,

Just good friends. Sharing a cuddle with Troy Corser. Ahhh... (Gold & Goose)

Donington Park in April. It snowed during practice, so the jacket was an essential piece of kit. Team coordinator Havier Beltran agrees. (Gold & Goose)

apparently offered greater rigidity at the rear which improved tyre life. Slight also felt that it gave much better feel for rear-wheel traction. Thanks to the new rear-end, the old double-stack exhaust system on the left-hand side was gone, in its place a twin-exit system with an end-can routed either side of the swing-arm and finishing high up not far from the tail unit. This gave the machine greater ground clearance and the chief mechanics a greater choice of ride-height settings. By this stage in its development, the RC45 steered well and was plenty fast, thanks in part to a new twin-injector system on each cylinder. One problem for Slight and Edwards was a bit of a carry-over from 1997. During the previous season, Kocinski and Slight had experimented with a Racing Dual Combined Braking System. Like the single-sided swing-arm, this was more of a marketing nod to the Dual CBS road system, which appeared on a number of Honda road bikes. The system effectively introduced a little back brake when you pulled the front brake lever. Kocinski had flatly refused to use the system, but Slight persevered with it for a while before adopting a more

traditional set-up. During testing for 1998 it was found that the Brembo brakes on the RC45 were dragging on a little. Whether or not this was a throwback from the old CBS system or not, it took Slight half the season to track down the problem. He was the more afflicted by it of the two riders.

During the off-season, Slight had worked hard on his fitness. He knew he was favourite to lift the title. Edwards, meanwhile, had an operation…

When Edwards finally got to test the RC45, he was knocked out by the V4's power and torque. 'Even after just rolling out of the pitlane, I knew why I never beat the Honda. It was impressive,' he says.

The first round again visited the glorious curves of Phillip Island, a track on which Edwards and the Yamaha had shone. But how would things go with the switch to Honda power?

Not at all well. A brace of seventh places was not what Colin wanted, although at least he was consistent. Slight was down in ninth in race one after a clash with Jean-Marc Deletang. The Kiwi was battling for third with Haga when the pair came upon the Frenchman. Haga

91

Win number one. Monza sees Colin finally achieve an important psychological goal. (Gold & Goose)

Check out the style. Different bike, same precision. Colin on the RC45. (Gold & Goose)

Which is backed up hours later by a second victory. Colin shows off his silverware. (Gold & Goose)

went up the inside, while Slight went round the outside. Deletang picked up his YZF, forcing Aaron onto the grass and down he went. He remounted to salvage some points. Many riders were having problems battling the blustery conditions, which made it difficult for them to hold a line through corners. Slight made amends with a second in race two, but the real story was Haga. After third in race one he succeeded in race two where other Japanese riders had failed. He proved that 1997's victory wasn't a flash in the pan. He could win at other tracks and so could the old YZF.

Many would say this was a bit embarrassing for Colin, the rider who'd been telling everyone how much better the RC45 was than the YZF. Edwards was adamant, though, that he would be proved right in the long run.

Even the way Haga won the race, battling with Slight in an almost carbon copy of the Slight-Edwards clash in 1997, was telling. Haga took the win where Edwards could not, staving off the supposedly superior Honda to win the race by seven one hundredths of a second.

In round two Haga turned up at a decidedly wintery Donington Park, never having seen the place before. After battling with WSB-returnee Corser in both races, he took the double. That was a first for the Yamaha and gave Haga his third straight win. It also gave him a 21-point lead over Corser in the championship.

How could this happen on a five-year-old machine which the combined talents of Edwards, Russell, et al had failed to win on? And why hadn't Edwards shone on the RC45? First, Colin was coming off the back of a lengthy lay-off and hadn't raced for many months. Second, the improvements made to the YZF would have benefited him if he had stayed with the Belgarda team. For 1998 the YZF had winter updates in the form of new pistons and camshafts with more overlap and longer valve timing. Good power now came in at 8,000rpm like in 1997, with the rev-limiter cutting in at 14,300rpm.

More mid-range came courtesy of a new Akrapovic four-into-one exhaust. Strangely, Haga's team-mate Russell was using Michelin tyres while Haga was on Dunlops. Ultimately, who's to say that if Edwards had been fit to race at the end of 1997 or had still been on the YZF in 1998 he wouldn't have taken his maiden win? Either way, he was convinced he'd made the right decision, even after the poor showing in the first race meeting of the 1998 season. 'I know I didn't win a race on it and Haga did,' says Edwards, 'but he eventually found the same thing. Yeah, he could win at tracks like Donington Park, Phillip Island and Sugo, but at other places he'd be nowhere, just like anyone else on the Yamaha.'

Meanwhile, Edwards was working hard with new crew chief Gorst to build a winning relationship – essential for any machine development.

After three seasons in the top flight of four-stroke racing, Edwards had to start to shine. He was on the machine that had won the previous year's championship and he was behind his illustrious team-mate in the championship.

Monza was the turning point. Glory and sadness all encapsulated in one race meeting. Saturday practice in the Supersport championship saw the death of Michael Paquay in a multiple pile-up. The Belgian was riding a Honda CBR600 alongside young Brit James Toseland in the Castrol Honda squad. Haga, meanwhile, was in the wars after suffering a massive high-side in practice. The battered and bruised Japanese rider struggled into 15th place during the new-for-1998 Superpole flying practice lap. Slight qualified on pole at the fast circuit, while Edwards was third. The scene was set. Fogarty led into the first, notorious chicane, closely followed by Slight and Corser. Soon Slight made it past while Edwards was also making up places. The final few laps were a Castrol Honda-only affair. Slight got his RC45 squirming into the final Parabolica corner, only for Edwards to take a slightly wider line and hit the apex of the corner a few inches ahead of the Kiwi veteran. They crossed the line drafting a backmarker and, after 48 WSB starts, Edwards crossed the line just 0.083 of a second ahead. He'd finally won his first WSB race and the ghosts of Phillip Island the year before were banished.

In race two the confident Honda pair were expected to dominate again. After a typical Monza

Laguna was a disappointing experience in 1998 with 11th and 10th places. (Gold & Goose)

melee in the early laps the pair broke through again and made the race their own.

Crossing the line for the penultimate time, Slight was snicking into top gear when his bike let go in dramatic fashion, as the V4 motor dropped a rod. He parked up the flaming Honda and kissed goodbye to 20, or maybe 25 points.

Slight's break down was typical of his luck that year. 'If it wasn't for bad luck, I wouldn't have any luck at all,' he said. At Donington Park he'd even suffered a misfire while chasing Fogarty, which was later traced to broken wire in the RC45's wiring loom.

Neil Tuxworth reflected on his Superbike riders' contrasting fortunes. 'It was sad for Aaron as he was on a certain second place at least; it could have even been first for him. It's so rare for the Honda to suffer a failure like that. It's only the second such failure in five seasons of racing with the RC45.'

With a comfortable cushion to the chasing Ducatis, Edwards crossed the line to record a notable double. He'd won on the RC45 in only his third meeting on the bike and matched a feat achieved by Foggy but not yet Slight – a double on the once recalcitrant RC45. He

celebrated with a massive burnout. Edwards leapfrogged Slight into fourth place in the championship standings thanks to his 50-point haul.

'Those first wins confirmed what I thought,' says Colin. 'I knew I had the talent and the ability, but by then I also had the experience and the ability to work with the team and the people within it.'

Albacete played host to the next round. Race one was held in awful weather conditions and the 'normal' race order in the Castrol team was resumed. Slight took fourth ahead of Edwards and behind local hero and privateer Ducati rider Gregorio Lavilla. Chili took the win, Corser was second and Foggy languished down in ninth as a result of his crash in the new Superpole. Race two saw Foggy take the win in much improved conditions, but Edwards was involved in a first lap pile-up, which meant no points. Slight came second.

Things improved for Colin in the next round at the Nürburgring. In race one the Castrol Honda boys had it all their own way. The wily old Slight got the better of Edwards in the wet conditions to take his first win of the year. Rain delayed race two, then Chili took the lead, leaving the Honda duo to scrap it out. Slight

Back on the top of the rostrum at Brands. (Gold & Goose)

moved into second and looked to be catching Chili until he slid off with six laps to go. With the warning plain to see, Colin backed off; Aaron remounted to take fourth. Corser now led the series never having won a race. Chili and Slight were tied on points in second ahead of early leader Haga, while Edwards was in fifth. Foggy – behind Colin in the standings – had one of his poorest showings for years with a brace of 13th placings.

Before 1997 it would have been inconceivable – a Honda double at Misano, Ducati's backyard. Worse still for Ducati (which tests at the track), last year's wins for Kocinski and Slight were backed up by another double. It was all the more remarkable that the double winner was Slight, his first ever. The haul put him within six points of Corser in the championship, while Edwards's third and fourth jumped him into third ahead of Foggy. First doubles were the name of the game in 1998, with Chili taking his first in round seven at Kyalami, South Africa – the first time the WSB paddock had visited the continent since the end of Apartheid.

Everyone struggled on a track for which they had no data and which, at 5,000ft above sea level, starved engines of vital oxygen. The Castrol Honda boys could only finish eighth and ninth in race one. Slight got the better of Edwards on this occasion, but Edwards improved in the second encounter, taking a fourth to Slight's second eighth place of the day.

Two massive accidents marred a black meeting at Edwards's home round of Laguna Seca. There were no strong showings from the official Honda WSB team either, despite Kocinski's double the year before. Edwards finished 11th in the first race and tenth in the second. Slight's results were affected by crashes. Race one was stopped after a hideous smash at the top of the Corkscrew. Doug Chandler's Muzzy Kawasaki went down when a clip-on handlebar snapped and he smashed into Akira Yanagawa as he committed himself to the notorious turn. The crash would put the Japanese rider out of the next meeting at Brands Hatch. A second crash at the restart was even more sickening. Aaron Yates's Yoshimura Suzuki clashed handlebars with Slight's Honda. The result was battered bodies lying motionless. It looked more like a

war zone than a race grid. Slight was injured and the result was taken from the end of the 12th lap. He failed to start race two.

Things improved dramatically at Brands. The 82,000-strong crowd saw the Castrol Honda pairing start third and fourth on the grid, with Edwards one better than his more experienced team-mate. Corser led the way into Paddock Hill Bend for the first time, but soon the Hondas got past and pulled away. Edwards had the edge over Aaron, who was still suffering from his Laguna crash although, as his performance was proving, it wasn't a problem on the bike. Aaron closed the gap in the final few laps, but Edwards managed to hold on to the lead through Clearways and on to the flag. Aaron was happy to close the points gap on Corser at the top of the championship standings, while Edwards passed Chili in the points for fourth overall. In race two Edwards again beat his team-mate, this time with the Hondas coming home in fourth and fifth.

When the WSB circus arrived at the A-1 Ring (no, not the most imaginatively titled track in the world) Slight had some catching up to do; he was 30.5 points

Sugo, and Colin wasn't in contention to help team-mate Aaron Slight to the title. (Gold & Goose)

Storm warning: Colin warned of ten wins in 1999. (Gold & Goose)

down on series leader Corser. The double he got at the track near Zeltweg in Austria was just what the doctor ordered, closing him to within a point-and-a-half of Corser overall. Edwards wasn't so happy, finishing the weekend with a seventh and ninth, and letting Chili back into fourth overall.

At Assen the bunching up at the top of the championship came second to the 'real' story of Chili and Fogarty's very public falling out. The Italian had won the first race ahead of the Briton, with Corser third ahead of Slight. Edwards battled with the Yamahas of Russell and Haga early on before breaking clear to follow his team-mate home. In race two the fireworks started. Foggy and Chili led the last few laps, duking it out on the fast curves, before Chili led going into the final chicane. Foggy outbraked Chili and the Italian went down. According to Pierfrancesco, Foggy made a couple of blocking passes which he was not happy with and told him so by making a very public appearance in his towelling bath robe at the post-race press conference. It was an ugly scene. With Chili disqualified for being pushed across the line by fans, Slighty took second ahead of Corser and Edwards. The championship race

was alive for the final round at Sugo.

The three-horse race between Corser, Slight and Foggy became a two horse one on race morning. Corser crashed in warm-up and broke three ribs, damaging his spleen in the process. Castrol Honda's challenge for the championship failed to materialise, possibly because of tyres that just didn't seem to work on the V4 at Sugo. Edwards languished down in 13th place in race one, while Slight battled with Neil Hodgson's Kawasaki to finish behind the Briton in seventh. The pair then had an hilarious 'hand bags at 20 paces' stand-off on the slow-down lap. Apparently Slight had asked Hodgson to let him through, but the Englishman (who was battling for a job in 1999) was loathe to do so. Race two, the last of the year, ended as the season began. Haga took the win. Fogarty's fourth place gave him the title. Slight managed sixth, while Edwards again languished in 13th, behind Russell. Tyres were the issue for the Hondas – any Hondas. Slight and Edwards were the highest-placed Hondas, with the home riders struggling even more.

Despite a shaky start, by the end of 1998 Edwards's decision to move to Honda proved to be right. He

finished ahead of both factory Yamahas in fifth place; Haga came just behind in sixth. There wasn't any shame in finishing behind Slight, who came second in the series – only the talented Kocinski had bettered the Kiwi in the team-mate stakes in five seasons at Castrol Honda. Instead it boded well for 1999, even if there were still a few machine problems to sort out.

'The front suspension on the RC45 was still a problem; it was never perfect at every track. For 1999 I knew I was going to have to learn and adapt the machine to the way I wanted it,' says Edwards.

He had also integrated well into the team. 'He was superb to work with,' says team boss Tuxworth. He was so easy going and the easiest rider to work and get on with. Even after winning races and later championships he never got big-headed, he always appreciated that it was the work of the whole team as well. He's never changed as a person. I once said to him, as a joke of course, "Colin, you're a very nice bloke for an American…"'

For 1999 the nice bloke had to go. Nothing less than a full-on attempt at the championship would do.

Slight recognised the change in Edwards. In his autobiography, *You Don't Know The Half Of It*, he says: 'Colin was becoming more and more aggressive. I noticed his new attitude in the pit. If there was a test session where I was faster than him, he'd keep on trying and trying to better my time. With Adrian firing him up, it was as if he always had to be the fastest Honda rider out there.'

Edwards wanted to continue his improvement and changes to the RC45 were helping.

'The bike is much better than last year,' explained Edwards at the time. 'The biggest improvement was in the suspension. Once we'd got that figured out it felt like a whole different motorcycle. From early testing in 1999 you could actually lose the front and get it back; before you couldn't do that. Most of my 1998 crashes were when I lost the front. For 1999 I don't wanna be fighting for fourth or fifth or even podium places. Winning and the championship are the only things for me.'

But during testing at Laguna Seca, two weeks before the opening race of the season, he tore shoulder muscles that would restrict his ability to muscle the chunky RC45 around.

Always up for a scrap, Colin battles with Haga and Slight at the title opener in Australia. He'd get two thirds. (Gold & Goose)

Leading Foggy at Donington's Esses before winning race two. (Gold & Goose)

Round one was back at Kyalami in South Africa. Edwards and Slight were a strong team on paper, certainly as strong as the Ducati dream-team of Fogarty and Corser. Yamaha finally had a new machine in the shape of the YZF-R7, the OW-02, in the hands of Haga and Vito Guareschi. The machine was a beautiful piece of kit, but exactly how much development work was required before it became a winner was unclear. Also, after seasons on his favoured Dunlops, Haga was on Michelins.

Another new machine was Aprilia's Mille, ridden by Peter Goddard. It looked good, but would need developing. Probably more so than the Yamaha. Kawasaki, now on the last carburated machine on the grid, had Akira Yanagawa riding again. He was joined by the previous year's impressive Ducati privateer Gregorio Lavilla. Suzuki lost the Harris-run team of Jamie Whitham and Goddard, to be replaced by Chili in an Alstare team sponsored by Corona beer. He was joined by Japanese rider Katsuaki Fujiwara.

In the opening race of the season Fogarty and Corser made the break, closely followed by Haga.

Edwards was back in fourth. Slight soon made up the time from his fluffed start to pass Edwards and Haga to take third behind winner Fogarty and second-placed Corser. Haga eventually beat Edwards, who was still in some pain, into fourth. Foggy completed the double in race two, although second and third were reversed with Slight taking second and Corser third, ahead of Edwards.

Phillip Island saw a distinct lack of gulls compared with previous years, but the racing was as close as ever. Corser was on pole, followed by Carl, Aaron and Edwards. Fifth was 250 GP refugee Doriano Romboni on the development Ducati.

As Troy ran away with race one, Edwards battled with Foggy, before being embroiled in a big battle for third with Slight, Haga and Yanagawa. It was classic Phillip Island stuff and Edwards managed to get the better of Slight for third, while the Kiwi fended off the Yamaha and Kawasaki riders for fourth. In race two Edwards got his first podium of the year, beating Slight and Haga in an exciting battle for third. The Ducati Performance team had won all four races in the first two meetings of the year, Foggy doing the double at

Back at Monza, but only two second places in 1999. (Gold & Goose)

More disappointment came at home. Again. (Gold & Goose)

Back at Brands and winning again. (Graeme Brown)

Kyalami and Troy doing the same on 'The Island'. All this was about to change in round three.

In fact, Donington Park was the end of an era, of sorts, the end of a friendship between Slight and Edwards.

Chili took the first pole position of his career on the Alstare-Corona Suzuki, but in the race after it all settled down with Foggy taking the win, followed by Slight, Edwards and British wild-card Chris Walker in fourth. Race two was where the action was. First, Goddard high-sided his Aprilia on the exit of the double apex of Coppice. Corser looked as if he was running away with it, while Chili battled with Edwards and Slight. The Kiwi performed a mammoth outbraking move up the inside of Edwards into the Melbourne Loop only to drift wide, letting the Texan back up the inside. Slight stuck to his wide line, possibly in an attempt to get out of the corner ahead of his team-mate, while Edwards held his line then began to drift out a little – nothing unusual coming out of Melbourne so you can fire the bike up the hill towards Goddards. But, with Slight not giving an inch, he had nowhere to go other than off the kerb and onto the grass. Perhaps finally realising what was happening, Edwards looked over his shoulder as Slight crashed. Slight wasn't amused. He got up and flicked a single finger at Edwards on his departing RC45. Edwards was now battling with Foggy for second and both were catching Corser. Edwards's body language on the bike showed complete confidence in his machine, as he hauled up on the RC45's fiercesome brakes to go up the inside of Foggy at Goddards. He even had time to wave at Foggy going down the start-finish straight.

Edwards was on a roll and slipped through on Corser at McLeans, with Foggy following him through. More inter-team drama followed when Slight, who went into the pits to get his damaged bike fixed, prepared to be lapped by once more showing his displeasure with his team-mate.

It didn't help the Kiwi, who crashed out again at McLeans, perhaps thanks to the injury he'd received to his little finger and hand in the original crash. Edwards took his first win of the season, taking him to third overall ahead of Slight.

So what of the race win Colin?

'After the first race I figured we could have been up there. We knew we had the race bike to do it, it was just a matter of being up there and doing it. That was awesome, just the perfect race.'

Privately, even Foggy said that if Edwards hadn't had the problems he had in race one, then the chances were the Texan would have scored a double.

Behind the scenes, things weren't good in the Castrol Honda team. Slight was convinced that Edwards had done it deliberately. The media scrutiny was intense. 'The only reason people are interested in the crash,' said Edwards at the time, 'is because we're on the same make of bike.' Edwards most definitely saw it as a racing incident – nothing more. In Slight's autobiography, he says: 'That night Colin comes to my motorhome, smiling. He said: "Did you see that as a racing incident?" By this time I had replayed the incident on video and was facing the prospect of losing my finger. I said: "That's not what happened, you deliberately ran me off the racetrack." It really pissed me off that he just went straight into how he felt it was a racing incident. There was no concern about my finger, he just wanted to offload his guilt by trying to convince himself it was a racing incident.'

Slight claimed that at the time, team boss Neil Tuxworth wouldn't make a call on who was to blame or that he hadn't watched the incident on video.

In retrospect, Tuxworth has this to say. 'Aaron hit Colin from behind unfortunately. I don't believe and I still maintain that I don't think Colin even saw Aaron. I sat and studied it frame-by-frame in race control and you can see Aaron was behind Colin when Colin simply went wide. Aaron was furious, as we know. It was just a racing incident.'

Either way, it affected the season big time. Slight was now injured for the next round, but would ride with the damaged finger, rejecting an amputation, a typical racing 'quick-fix'.

One thing the race at Donington Park did was show what the British public thought of Edwards. They liked him a lot. Like Foggy, he said what he thought – there was no BS with CE. When the fuss died down,

Edwards was third in the championship, ahead of Aaron by 15 points.

Edwards qualified second on the grid for round four at Albacete in Spain. Despite getting a good start he was forced to run off the track with a mechanical problem while Slight bravely battled to fourth. Race two saw Aaron slide to seventh, while Edwards battled with Foggy, Yanagawa and Haga, with the Japanese rider looking particularly loose on the new R7. Edwards took the win, using a backmarker to his advantage to keep Yanagawa and Fogarty at bay. Edwards was starting to threaten Corser for second in the series. He was just nine points behind the Australian as the party headed to Monza, a track at which Edwards was traditionally strong.

Race one and Edwards lined up on pole, but he was forced to chase early leader Corser, who got a flyer off the line into the first chicane. Fogarty, Romboni and Edwards took off in pursuit along with Slight. Romboni suffered a nasty accident after a coming-together with Slight, when the Italian trapped his leg between the tyre and his bike.

Soon Foggy, Edwards and Chili were catching Corser.

Flashing across the line Edwards outbraked both Ducatis into the first chicane as Corser bumped over the kerb. As Foggy and Edwards came out of the Parabolica for the last time, Foggy managed to draft past to win by a tenth of a second. Edwards – completely at odds with his normal easy-going self – was angry and almost inconsolable at coming second, and threw water over a TV camera. Later, on the podium with Chili and Foggy, there were more fireworks as he'd asked Chili not to spray champagne into his eyes because it stung. Edwards threw his bottle down in a huff and it smashed into a thousand pieces.

Was the easy going dude turning into a tantrum thrower now that he felt he should be winning more races?

If you think a tenth of a second is close in racing, then race two was closer still.

There was more bad news for Aaron. He was penalised for a jump start, but didn't see or ignored the calls for him to come in and was black flagged. Not

And celebrating
big style on
the podium.
(Graeme Brown)

good as a camera crew from New Zealand were in Europe at the time to follow his progress. Again, it would be Edwards, Foggy and Chili battling it out, as the Italian showed what a force the GSX-R750 could be in the right hands. On the last lap it looked as if Edwards had it won as Foggy clipped and jumped over the opposite kerb on the exit of the second chicane. This gave Edwards a precious four- or five-bike-length advantage and Chili the chance he needed to snap past the Englishman. Foggy coolly passed Chili a few corners later and set off after Edwards. Down the back straight Foggy tried to hang on to the Honda's slipstream, but it was Edwards that led into the Parabolica. Despite the new finish line that year being closer to the exit of the corner – therefore favouring the rider coming out of the corner first – Foggy simply used a small slingshot off Edwards's RC45 to pull up on the outside. The pair crossed the line almost side-by-side. Both riders were nonplussed as they crossed the line. The electronic timing equipment first gave the race to Edwards, only for a race version of an electoral recount to give the race to Carl by just five-thousandths of a second.

You'd think it was prime time for Edwards to be even more upset, but this time in the post-race interviews he was more reflective.

'I'd just like to apologise to all the fans and people at home on the TV for being an asshole after that first race…'

Foggy now led the championship by 55 points from Edwards, who appeared to be the biggest threat to the Englishman winning the title.

The Nürburgring was to provide more drama and tantrums for Edwards although this time he had good reason. He started the first race second on the grid and led from the start.

Early in the first race Igor Jerman's Kawasaki blew up on the racing line down the start-finish straight, and although leader Fogarty went through okay, Yanagawa went down, obviously thanks to the oil deposited by Jerman's ZX-7R. Foolishly the German race officials didn't hang out the oil flags, so the next time the leaders came round, both Edwards and Chili nearly went down. The following lap and Haga's R7 gets all

crossed up and goes straight into the gravel, to be followed a lap later by Chili going down. By now the pits are in pandemonium. Davide Tardozzi – despite the fact that his two riders were in the lead – asked for the race to be stopped, as did Honda's Neil Tuxworth. Meanwhile, Chili, back in the pits, threatened race control with legal action for loss of earnings for their lack of action with the flags.

Flags and their lack of movement was a big issue. Foggy, leading the race, came up on a backmarker and promptly knocked him off. The unhorsed rider got up and berated the marshals for not waving the blue flag, which indicates to slower, lapped riders that a faster bike is approaching. A further five laps later, Edwards went down on the oil. He was livid, immediately got to his feet and threw a handful of gravel on the track, before he turned on the marshals' post and stuck the middle fingers of both hands up at the luckless men. He even gave a medical marshal the brush-off.

This hurt Edwards title hopes hard. Race two didn't help. Edwards riding seemed much more subdued. Some felt that he'd lost his concentration but he still finished fourth in the race. Either way, Edwards had had it with the German officials who had run the show.

'I'm not fucking coming back to this country,' he said. He would, but the WSB circus would not return to the Nürburgring.

Misano saw a downturn in Edwards's fortunes, when he bagged a sixth and seventh, behind each of his championship rivals. Laguna saw another home rider benefit, with Australian Anthony Gobert taking his domestic Vance & Hines Ducati to a race one win while team-mate Ben Bostrom secured race two. Edwards, with his fourth and fifth places, made points up on second-placed Corser in the standings.

Brands Hatch was the scene of another remarkable double for Edwards. As soon as the lights turned green he led the way, closely followed by his Castrol Honda team-mate Slight. The pair weren't headed. Race two saw another double double for the Castrol Honda squad. Edwards and Slight battled it out, closely followed by Chili, before the Italian's rear Dunlop de-laminated and simultaneously shredded his chances of a finish. As the pair hit the compression at the bottom of Paddock Hill on the slow down lap, they both shook hands, showing that, in public at least, they had buried the hatchet.

The A-1 Ring was damp, and again Chili, Slight and Edwards were up front. Chili passed Slight and Edwards to lead, only to crash out when he was riding two seconds a lap faster than anyone else. Both Slight and Corser took turns to lead before both crashed out and Edwards tip-toed around the track on a slick tyre to sneak the win. Race two saw Chili take the GSX-R750's first win outside of Japan in another wet display, while Edwards came eighth.

Assen proved to be another Fogarty benefit race, with Corser scooping two seconds and Slight both thirds. With just two fifth places for Colin, third was looking likely in the championship. Then at Hockenheim, Corser had a bad weekend, DNFing in race one and finishing seventh in the second leg. Edwards made up ground with a fourth and fifth. Slight's bad luck continued with his race one win being disallowed because of a red flag, which meant results

were put back one lap to before he'd passed Fogarty. It didn't affect the end result. Foggy was crowned champion again.

Compared with the previous year, the 1999 season-ender in Sugo was a lacklustre affair. Japanese riders made up the bulk of the top ten, with Edwards's two ninth places helping him to equal points with Corser. It would be Edwards who would wear the number two plate in 2000, though, as he scored more race wins – five to the Australian's three.

At the beginning of the 1999 season Slight had tested a development version of a new twin-cylinder race bike for HRC alongside Edwards on his RC45. When Slight recorded an identical time to Edwards, it was decided to develop the twin for competition in WSB for 2000.

At the end of the year, deals weren't finalised for 2000, but it was obvious Honda wanted to keep hold of the young Texan. He said: 'I would love to stay. It would be the biggest thrill in the world to be on the Honda twin and race Carl for the championship. It would be a new challenge.'

Two ninths at Sugo, but a countback of wins meant he'd taken second in the series ahead of Troy Corser. (Gold & Goose)

An (eventual) double at Kyalami was the perfect start, although Noriyuki Haga's banned substance scandal would continue to the end of the season. (Gold & Goose)

World champion

Edwards entered the new millennium on a racing high. In 1999 he'd made a brash boast about winning ten races that year. He didn't, but it gave some indication of his confidence and, besides, finishing second behind Carl Fogarty wasn't such a bad result.

But second place isn't good enough if you want to be a winner and Honda was fed up with the dominant red twins getting the lion's share of the championship. So if they couldn't beat them with a four, they'd join them with a twin.

Aaron Slight had tested the VTR the previous season, but in the winter of 1999 it was down to Edwards to shoulder the responsibility of developing the bike. The Kiwi suffered from a mystery illness, which left him finding it hard to concentrate. The condition had dogged his 1999 campaign.

'I kind of developed the VTR,' Edwards says. 'Me and Aaron had different ideas of what we wanted from a motorcycle, but he had a lot of experience with the RC45 and we were both shooting for the same goals. The SP-1 feels slower than the RC45 and it's not so violent. It's really smooth and powerful. With the V4 and four cylinders, you're worried about where you've just been because it tried to kill you. With this thing, you can just concentrate on where you're going... You can slide it real smooth, especially on corners, while the four cylinders are just a bit fast.'

Slight was drooling at the prospect of riding a Honda twin against the Ducati hordes. He'd been one of the most vocal about the rules, which seemed to favour the machines from Bologna. 'There's always another fuckin' jerk on a Ducati,' he said in 1996 as he

They started testing the SP-1 as team-mates looking at being together for the third straight season, but Aaron's poor health meant Colin would spend the early part of 2000 without him. (Gold & Goose)

struggled to get the RC45 working consistently at all tracks on the WSB calendar. Sadly, Aaron would never get a proper shot at the title. Just weeks before the first race of the season, his illness was diagnosed. The Kiwi had a 2cm bleed in his brain caused by a congenitally weak blood vessel, which, unbeknown to him, had burst. He was back for Donington Park just 12 weeks after brain surgery, but he wouldn't be able to shoot for the title.

So who could? Colin was under no doubts as to his main rival.

'Carl's the man to beat, obviously,' he said at the time, 'and Haga will be right in there. You can never count that guy out, although some people have because he hasn't been going super-fast in the off-season. That's just Haga: he has a real hard time getting motivated during testing and it shows. Once the light turns green he'll be a threat to win any race he enters. The Yamaha turns so well, it's beautiful really. Whether he can bring all that together to win the title, I don't know. The Kawasakis will maybe win the odd race but not the championship. Troy Corser on the Aprilia? An uphill battle for sure, but you'll see more from that bike in the next few months than you ever have before. Pierfrancesco Chili on the Suzuki did pretty well in 1999, I thought. Always is a threat to win races, but has never made a championship run work for him yet. Will he this year? I doubt it.'

The first of two interesting new additions to the series was Ben Bostrom, an ex-AMA champion with Honda, then moving from the Vance & Hines Ducati AMA team where he won a WSB race as a wild card in 1999. What did 2000 hold for Ben?

'This will be a pretty hectic year for Ben,' Edwards said in 2000. 'He's used to AMA where the whole thing comes down to who gets the good tyre, and where the amount of tyres and equipment for the bike that gets thrown at you is pretty limited. From now on he's going to see 18 different rear tyres at the first race, with ten different fork and shock combinations, and he has to find something in there that will work. Plus learn the tracks, and learn how to work with that team.'

Replacing Slight at Castrol Honda was another talented Kiwi, ex-Kawasaki WSB regular and 500cc GP

winner Simon Crafar. 'I know how good the bike is so there are no questions there. He seems to have a problem with Michelin tyres, but if he can get past that he will be at the front,' said Edwards.

One of the biggest surprise packages for 2000 was Anthony Gobert on a Suzuki-powered Bimota SB-8R in a team with Levi denim jeans backing [which never transpired] run by ex-Ducati favourite son Virginio Ferrari. 'Well, nobody has been able to control him for an entire season yet,' said Edwards, 'so I'm not sure that Bimota will be able to. Virginio Ferrari might be a guy who can do better in that department than others, but Gobert is still Gobert. Something is going to happen; you know that. And it's probably not going to be good.'

The VTR was untried. No machine had won the WSB in its debut year since 1994 and the Ducati 916. Could Honda do it? The machine was pumping out a claimed 165bhp, which was probably bang on as the bike proved to be pretty rapid through the speed traps. Weight was another area where the Honda had no problems. The machine rolled on to the grid for the

Gunnin' for the
title in Japan...
(Gold & Goose)

Working out the
intricacies of
the VTR with
Gorst in Italy...
(Gold & Goose)

...before playing
chicken with
Monza's many
chicanes.
(Gold & Goose)

first race of the season equipped with an electric start, which was Honda's idea, rather than a brutal roller starter which could be tough on the drivetrain.

Kyalami, South Africa, and round one of the new season proved to be the (almost) perfect start for Edwards, with a win in race one and a second in race two. Haga was sparkling on the improved Yamaha R7, while Corser proved his Aprilia Superpole was no fluke with fourth and third places – the Mille's first rostrum. Foggy, battling with a pre-season shoulder injury, clawed his way on to the rostrum in race one, then fell chasing the leaders in race two.

It was after the racing that the political farce kicked in.

Haga had tested positive for the banned substance ephedrine. He claimed it must have been in an herbal weight-loss formula he'd been taking to lose some excess baggage he'd been carrying in previous seasons, but that he had no idea it was in the concoction. The drug is favoured by weight lifters, where it can help dissolve fat and stimulate the brain, in a similar way to Speed.

Thanks to bans, appeals and counter appeals, the fall out would last all the way from April to the final round at Brands Hatch in October. The WSB powers that be would not come out of this at all well…

At round two at Phillip Island variable weather threw up a couple of amazing results and – ultimately – the last hurrah of the greatest WSB racer ever. Anthony Gobert took race one. The mercurial wild-man used local knowledge and full wets to take the win ahead of a tiptoeing Foggy. In race two Corser gave Aprilia its debut win, again from pole position. Haga (racing under appeal) was second after a dismal tenth in the first race. But even these amazing results were overshadowed by the crash that put Carl Fogarty into retirement. A collision between the four-time champion and back marker Robert Ulm resulted in a horrible break to Foggy's upper left arm. The chance of a third title in a row was punted off into the Phillip Island dirt. Despite only managing two fifth places down under, Edwards was now the man most likely to

win the series. Foggy was gone, Haga was subject to a ban – and loss of points – and Slight was still recuperating from major surgery. Only Corser could put up some form of resistance, sitting in second place at the end of the second round with 54 points to Edwards's 72. Surely the Aprilia couldn't mount a consistent title challenge? For that matter, could the Honda?

'I think that because we won that first race at Kyalami,' says Colin, 'we had to keep winning just to impress people.'

Round three at Sugo was specialists' time. Hitoyasu Izutsu took a brace of wins on the pensionable Kawasaki ZX-7R. These were to be the last WSB victories for the venerable machine. Edwards's fifth and third gave him a useful 20-point cushion over Haga in the title chase, while Troy Bayliss – making his debut for the factory Ducati squad in place of Foggy – didn't get a chance to shine after being punted off for a pair of DNFs. It mattered little, he'd soon shine. Donington and round four saw Edwards win race one, while Britons

Neil Hodgson and Chris Walker came to the fore. Hodgson got a third and a race win, and Walker steered his Suzuki to second place behind Hodgson in race two.

Edwards had been flying all weekend. In unofficial practice he'd stuck in a 1m 32.599s lap, which was inside Simon Crafar's 500cc GP lap record. With a race one win under his belt, he was pulling away going for the double when the front-end of his SP-1 folded, letting Chili through into the lead. One big plus point for Castrol Honda was the welcome return of Aaron Slight, just 12 weeks after major surgery. He scooped ninth and seventh places. A pair of fourths for Haga gave the Japanese rider a pre-penalty 11-point lead in the series. Ducati, meanwhile, was desperately trying to find a replacement for Foggy, drafting in the expensive and not very impressive Luca Cadalora, who could only manage a DNF and a 17th place.

The constant threat of Haga getting those 45 points back for his Kyalami showing must have been playing on Edwards's mind.

Colin was smooth as silk, especially in the wet.
(Gold & Goose)

Colin knew the value of knowing everything he could about the tyres. Michelin rates him as one of its best development riders – ever.
(Gold & Goose)

'For me it was simple,' he says. 'It made me push that much harder. I was pretty sure he wouldn't ultimately get his points back, but I just wanted to be enough points clear by the last race of the season so that even if he was given them back, it wouldn't matter.'

Round five was at Monza. Chili was magnificent, taking the first race win before promptly stripping off for the fans and throwing most of his kit into the crowd. Edwards was only a shade under three hundredths of a second down in an amazing photo finish, his dream of another double dashed again. In race two, though, he made amends, narrowly beating the Italian in a weekend in which the pair showed they were a class apart. These performances put Chili and the Suzuki into second overall for the title, with Haga stuttering to a DNF and a sixth.

The Yamaha rider came back with a bang at the next round at Hockenheim, where Bayliss scored his maiden WSB win. Yanagawa took second on the Kawasaki, while Haga netted third. He managed to go two better in the second race, winning from Edwards and Chili to give him the same overall points score as the Texan, should he be awarded the 45 points docked at Kyalami.

The seventh round of the series went to Misano. By now Ducati's domination at the track had waned; it was more a case of Corser blitzing the opposition to take Aprilia's first double. Edwards, meanwhile, took himself and his team-mate out of the first race (he held his hands up on this one, with Slight even making a joke about their coming together at Donington Park the year before). Race two was a stinker for Edwards, tenth behind Slight, which meant that Corser's double hauled him into second overall. This didn't account for Haga's extra points, who, despite being on a race ban, was actually racing subject to appeal.

Corser was now on a roll. Round eight went to Valencia for the first time and Troy won the first race, with Haga second. Again, Edwards suffered a lack of

In close company
with title
challenger Haga.
(Gold & Goose)

Hanging out
with Alyssia
in Laguna's
expansive
pit complex.
(Graeme Brown)

consistency, scoring a fifth and a fourth. What was going on?

'It was simple, the 2000 bike lacked consistency at all tracks, like the RC45, it was a bit hit and miss. It would work well at some tracks and not so good at others,' says Edwards.

Laguna Seca was little better. Second behind title challenger Haga was not what Edwards wanted in race one, while fourth against the Japanese rider's second again closed the gap 'in real terms' (i.e. with the 45 points docked) between the Honda and the Yamaha rider.

Brands Hatch and round ten would surely give the Texan some hope, it being one of his favourite tracks. But it wasn't to be. Race one was halted when Edwards clashed with Haga and Steve Hislop as the pack careered down Paddock Hill Bend. Hizzy was taken to hospital with a suspected broken neck. Thankfully, the injuries – while painful – were not that severe. After the restart Edwards could only manage

tenth, then a sixth in the second race. Haga, in contrast, got fifth and fourth places in another dominant display from the Britons (and honorary Britons), with Bayliss using the knowledge that helped him to the previous year's British Superbike title, while ex team-mate Hodgson took the second.

The Suzuka 8-Hour took place around the time of Brands. In the race itself Edwards crashed out, as did his team-mate Valentino Rossi, ruining their chances for the race. Surely all this flying around must tire racers out, almost to the point of exhaustion?

'I think you get used to it, if you possibly can,' says Edwards. 'I don't know what time zone I'm in anymore. If it's three o' clock in the day, if I'm tired, I'll sleep. I just try and get rest as much as possible. When I saw racers like Lawson, Schwantz and Rainey in interviews, I used to think "Damn, they look old" and they were only 30 or 31. And now I know why, because I'll be exactly the same when I'm 30 or 31. There's just not enough sleep and too much travel.'

Second and
fourth weren't
what Colin wanted
but this was
one of his best
US showings
for years.
(Gold & Goose)

British fans at
Assen missed
Foggy. They'd
come to love
Colin, with the
Texan being voted
the 2002 Man of
the Year by
*Motor Cycle
News* readers.
(Gold & Goose)

The title gap was now down to five points and it would become even closer at a rain-hit Assen. Edwards and Haga shared the wins, Colin winning the first and Haga the second, leaving both to share the top spot in the title race. Haga got the better of the points, taking a third behind Edwards in race one while Colin only managed fifth in race two.

If Edwards was going to win the championship, now was the time to stamp some sort of authority on it. He had to put the difficulties of the underlying politics firmly behind him and concentrate on the job in hand. He'd been racing for 22 years by the time he was lining up for the next two races. And very important they were, too.

'How do I prepare for a race?' says Edwards. 'I look around and learn and make my own assumptions. I've never gotten tired out on a bike. I've always had the attitude that this sport is so mentally draining but it's not so physically draining. You're mentally tough and you have to be, we travel to 13 to 14 different

countries in a year; if you're not mentally tough to keep the motivation and determination, then you're going to suffer. I think the biggest key is that I don't prepare any special way – eat rice or pasta. I don't do any of that. I just know that when I get on the bike, I'm faster than everybody else.'

Thankfully, HRC, Edwards and crew chief Adrian Gorst had also been making improvements to the VTR1000 SP-1. Honda being Honda, they'd spent the first part of the season trying to chase more outright horsepower on the twin. All this did was rob the bike of the twin's normal advantage – bottom end grunt – forcing Colin and Aaron to run higher revs as a result. For the next round at Oschersleben, Edwards would run higher gearing and this would give him the edge he needed. A win in Superpole, and two race wins in the penultimate round gave him 367 points. Haga, with only a ninth and a fifth for his troubles, was 32 points behind and with the hearing finally set for just prior to the last round of the series at Brands Hatch, it would take a political and riding miracle for the Japanese rider to take the title.

Wednesday, 11 October – just four days before the final round – saw the decision at the Court of Arbitration in Sport in Switzerland finally made for the transgressions in April in South Africa. Haga got back the 25 points for the race two Kyalami win, while his two-week ban was brought in with immediate effect on 12 October. Fans hoping for a title fight in the UK were to be disappointed.

The fight was over.

Brands in October isn't the place to guarantee good weather. And so it proved, with a wet, but rapidly drying race one giving old campaigner John Reynolds his debut WSB win. It was so nearly Edwards, who was catching Reynolds by a massive two seconds a lap, showing everyone that his poor Brands performance in the summer was forgotten following improvements to the bike. All that speed came to nothing when he fell while closing on the British wild-

card rider. He was rewarded with a raucous cheer from the fans, perhaps happier to see a British winner. In race two, Edwards was resplendent in some funky Spidi leathers to celebrate his title. This time no mistakes and some good fortune, when leader Hodgson retired with a mechanical problem before the final lap dust-up which the fans were looking forward to.

If it was an anti-climactic end to the season, it didn't matter. Edwards was world champion. He'd done it. Behind the scenes things had been tough.

'You get 100,000 people at Brands to watch and that's a lot of people,' says Edwards. 'That's pressure enough. Every race Castrol and Honda don't want you to finish second or third. They want the top step and that's enough pressure in itself... In the last race, I had a lot of family. I had probably 15 or 16 people from Texas come over, including my money manager, my travel agent, and other people. Unfortunately, one of my best friends [from home] had died two weeks before the race. He helped me improve my career. So Brands was

an emotional weekend, but I think any racer would tell you that the most pressure that he would have on himself is the pressure that he applies himself.'

One person who did see the pressure get to him was Edwards's long-time girlfriend, Alyssia. 'It's not normally stressful,' she says. 'But with the whole drug thing hanging over the results in 2000, it was. He also got real tired. So many races and flying around. He wasn't the same guy, no jokes or anything like that at all. He just sat around feeling tired. You could see his results suffer. I'm not into the politics but that hanging over the series for so long was bad. I started celebrating the title after Oschersleben, but Colin wouldn't until the last race in Brands. I'm just glad he won it by enough points to leave no doubt in anyone's mind that he should have been champ.'

With Foggy out early it was understandable that all eyes were on the guy carrying the number two plate.

'Everybody thought I'd win,' agrees Edwards. 'But we had to learn a brand new bike. In the end I didn't win as many races as I would have liked to. I wanted to win ten again, but ended up with eight. I was really focused that first weekend in South Africa to win the first race and once we did that, we got on the right foot. I guess after Foggy crashed, I thought I had it in the bag. That was a mistake. The season was a little bit turbulent. In the middle of the season, we kind of got off track so we tried a different motor with some different bits to it and at the end of the year, we got back to where we started more or less. My other team-mates had a difficult time with the bike but I got along with it from day one. You have to be smooth with the bike. That's the most important thing. You have to be really smooth and have finesse. Motorcycle-wise between the Honda and the Ducati, it was very close to things being equal. If anything, the Honda might be better on top-end, but bottom-end and mid-range I think it was pretty close to equal.'

Haga had put up a helluva fight, despite the drugs incident hanging over his head.

Lining up on pole at Oschersleben. His double win would effectively seal the title. (Gold & Goose)

Finally celebrating the 2000 World Superbike title after coming into the pits. (Gold & Goose)

And up on the
podium with
Adrian Gorst and
Neil Tuxworth.
(Gold & Goose)

Celebrating the
title back home
with a big
party.(Kel Edge)

'I think Haga had a point to prove after the drugs thing,' says Edwards. 'He wanted to show that it didn't take any of that to affect his performance. People love his wild, crazy riding. I don't, it's just not my style, but I love the guy to death and I'd never say a bad word about him.'

The championship meant a lot to Edwards, but to anyone who knows him he was still the same goofy guy.

'I saw a big change in the way some people treated me after the title. But I'm just a normal dude – Colin from Texas. I'm a normal guy that uses the same shitter as everybody else and puts my pants on one leg at a time just the same, too. A lot of the time, all I do is ride motorcycles a little better. That's it. A lot of people have a hard time getting around the fact that I am so approachable. I say what I think. I cuss at press conferences – and that's what I am. People want to know who you are so I don't tend to change anything about myself. I just do what I do.'

Cussing. Read the words in this book and you can't help spotting some cussing. But that's real-life.

That's Colin.

'In the beginning when I got with Honda I would slip up and say a few cuss words in TV interviews. When I say cuss words I mean that "shit" is about the worst thing I'm gonna say,' explains Edwards. 'Honda would say, "Well, you know... try not to cuss". This was like the first three or four months I was with them, but they finally realised "Hey, that's just him, that's the way he is".'

Everybody says the same. 'It's just Colin. He'll always be the same.' Tom Halverson, a friend from the old days and still a pal, says: 'That's the best thing about him. He's still the same as he ever was, there's no edge to him.'

Alyssia agrees. 'I think the reason we stayed together so long is down to the fact that Colin is just the same guy he was when we met. I met him before all this fame thing happened to him. He never takes anything for granted, which is part of the reason why I love him. He is always genuinely surprised when he sees the amount of interest he generates. I've seen so many people in the race business who as soon as they

Sign of the times. (Kel Edge)

Years of doing the best by his boy rewarded. A proud Senior, with Junior. (Kel Edge)

become famous they become assholes or treat people bad for no reason. Colin's not like that, he's just a normal guy who thinks about sex all the time! Just like any guy anywhere. He also still makes me laugh, which is important! He can throw a few tantrums, like at the Nürburgring, but I just tell him to stop acting like a child and a jackass.'

Alyssia has been a supporting influence ever since Edwards hit the world stage back in 1995.

'After a bad race you just have to be supportive,' she says. 'He'll come into the motorhome. I'll help him out of his leathers and he'll sit there for about 20 minutes and then say something about the race. That's when I'll mention it.'

And what about the stresses and strains of seeing her man being flung like a rag doll from a 170bhp superbike?

'Immediately I see him crash I'm thinking, "Oh my God, is he okay?" Then he gets up and I'm really pissed, thinking: "Why did you do that? We need those points, man!" I'm happy to sit in the garage and watch his race from there. I get so into his racing that

one time when Chris Vermeulen came past making a comment on what a nice sunny day it was and that it was a shame it wasn't hotter, I said to him: "No, we don't want it any hotter. The Michelin tyres don't work so well in the heat." Sad, huh?'

Downtime is important for Edwards. 'Relaxation for me is sitting on my couch at home, watching TV, flipping the remote. That's as good as it gets. A lot of people like to go on vacation to get away, but for me, whenever I'm home, I am away. A few people know what I do over in the States, but most don't. I like it like that.' Hobbies are mainly golf. And more golf. 'I used to be a bit of a golf widow,' says Alyssia. 'He'd go out all day, play golf and then come home. So I'd want to watch a movie or something in the evening and then the asshole would get out a patch of Astroturf and start practising his swing. And I'd go "Arggggh!" It made me so mad, so I decided to get into it myself. He said he wanted something for us both to do when he retired, so I'll play golf with him from time to time. You've got to do something together. We also do some wakeboarding and go bowling. I even tried riding a little

Getting down
at Kyalami.
(Graeme Brown)

Trying to second
guess the
weather with
team boss
Tuxworth at
Phillip Island.
(Graeme Brown)

Round one of
the 2001 season
and Colin proudly
displays the
number 1 plate
ahead of team-
mate Tadayuki
Okada.
(Graeme Brown)

Honda XR100 dirt bike, but I crashed into the only tree for miles around. We also got into rock climbing after Ben Bostrom did, although I was a little concerned after I heard that Ben got stuck on a mountain all night wearing nothing but shorts and a T-shirt.'

Don't be fooled. Anything Edwards attempts he digs deep and gives 110 per cent. In between dirt riding as a kid and taking up road racing, he played tennis. Well. Very well. One day Edwards went ten-pin bowling and simply lived and breathed it for three months, buying all the kit, until he was soon shooting regular 270s and 280s. The maximum score is 300.

It's a mirror image of his racing. Everything is a pursuit for perfection, however long it takes. Looking at a graph of Edwards's career, you'll see a slow steady climb to the top, as opposed to a contemporary like Troy Corser. Edwards and Troy both joined WSB full time in 1995 (Corser had a few one-off races in 1994). He won his first race in Austria the following year, but it wasn't until Colin was in his fourth WSB season that he won a race – the double at Monza. By this time Corser had won his first title, two seasons before. He's only two years older than Edwards and both are on top

of their respective games, but the difference in how they've got there is interesting. Troy, now with the Foggy Petronas team, is developing the FP-1 in a bid to secure that elusive second title.

'It felt good, y'know, to be world champion,' says Edwards. 'But for 2001 it was more a matter of basically realising that it was last year. It was a lot of hard work, but then you have to get on with the job and going about winning it again. A lot of people have been saying about how it puts me under a lot more pressure – being world champ and then trying to keep the title. I don't know if I think differently from a lot of them, but I've been working 20-odd years for one goal and that was to win the world title. To me the pressure is off – I've done it; I've accomplished my goal. From here on after is gravy, so I was looking to go out and win races and I knew I could.'

For one friend and experienced racer – Kevin Schwantz – perhaps Edwards was being a little too laid back during his title defence. 'I think it was soon after his first title,' says Schwantz. 'I saw him at Laguna and he was with some other guys trying to be a real clown prince. I kinda figured for a while that maybe he wasn't

Getting ready for the off at home while spanner-man Craig Burton does the business. (Graeme Brown)

taking his racing as seriously as he could have. In 2002 he eventually proved that nothing could have been further from the truth.'

The 2001 season dawned without Haga in the WSB paddock. He'd defected to GPs with the Red Bull Yamaha team. Edwards was to have a new team-mate, from 500cc GPs, no less than Tadayuki Okada, who had beaten Mick Doohan in a straight fight on the NSR500. Troy Bayliss looked to be the main threat, on the Ducati 998 F01. His team-mate was to be Ruben Xaus, a Spaniard from the Supersport class, while Ben Bostrom – who had an impressive end to the previous season – was in a separate L&M-sponsored team on Dunlops, not Michelin. Also on Ducatis (albeit older ones) was Hodgson, making a welcome return to WSB, with young James Toseland as his team-mate. Corser stayed with Aprilia, trying to find that little bit extra from the Mille to piece together a consistent title-threatening season.

Edwards's bike had changed a little for 2001. Again, Honda had tried to get more power from the twin, at the expense, as it turned out, of some reliability in the first couple of races.

Valencia and round one was a carbon copy of 2000, with Corser netting both wins. Edwards's sixth and fourth were not the start he wanted to his title defence.

Race one at Kyalami was more like it, with a win in race one. But in race two Edwards retired with 'electrical problems'. Okada had not scored in four races, suffering two similarly embarrassing problems. Strange, after a season and off-season of almost metronomic efficiency. 'I don't know what happened to the bike in race two but it just went kaput!' said Edwards at the time. 'I know it wasn't an electrical problem.'

The win was overshadowed by reports in a South African newspaper that Colin had said the continent would be better if you could 'nuke the townships'. It was a comment that was rigorously denied by Colin and the Castrol Honda team.

He put it all behind him for Phillip Island. The weather was atrocious, resulting in only one race being run. Edwards won and there were no more 'electrical problems'. At Sugo, and round four, the Michelin runners were in dire straits. Edwards was 12th and 13th,

with other factory riders on the French rubber fairing little better or much worse. Corser – on Dunlops – was galloping away with the title lead. By Monza Michelin's woes were forgotten, with Bayliss stamping his intentions on the championship with a brace of wins ahead of Edwards in both. Corser had a nightmare of a weekend – two DNFs saw him drop below Bayliss in the standings with Edwards just two points behind. Donington Park was normally kind to Colin, but fifth and sixth behind a few of the locals was again not the result he was looking for. Round seven at the Lausitzring saw Edwards take race one, with Bayliss snatching race two. Corser's title challenge was fading and it was looking like a Bayliss/Edwards showdown. It looked like Ducati had, at last, found a very capable Fogarty replacement.

At Misano the seesaw tipped in Bayliss's favour again, as Edwards's Michelins didn't seem to work as well in the 38°C heat. Third behind Bayliss and Bostrom in race one was followed by an off in race two. A red flag and restart saw Colin get back on to claim 11th. Bayliss was now 47 points ahead.

Laguna again wasn't what Edwards wanted. A double at home for Bostrom was part of the American's amazing run of five straight wins. Colin, meanwhile, was down to sixth in both legs. Bostrom kept it up at Brands, while Colin could manage no better than third and fifth. He seemed to be suffering from the old problem of consistency, while being ganged up on by the big boys from Bologna. Although spread thin, sometimes Ducati's tactics of flooding the grid worked. Meanwhile Edwards's team-mate was finding it hard to get on terms with the WSB old-hands.

Round 11 at Oschersleben gave some respite from the red menace with a win for Edwards in race one and a second behind Xaus, the Spaniard taking his first WSB win.

The penultimate round at Assen wouldn't have been the title decider, had it not been for some more tyre woes for Edwards. Third was the best he could do, suffering with instability from his front tyre. Worse was to follow. Gambling on a different front, which eventually promised more stability, equated to less speed and Edwards finished in tenth. It was a shame, as he was riding on the crest of a wave with his results in

Germany just a week before. The title went to Bayliss.

'It was our own fault,' admits Edwards. 'The only thing I lacked with the front tyre in the first race was a little stability at the end of the back straight. We went for another front, which we knew wouldn't turn quite so well, but would be more stable. It was a bad choice and cost me any chance of a win and the title.'

No one would work harder in 2002 to make sure the same thing didn't happen again. In the winter of 2001 and early 2002, Edwards would clock up about 12,000 miles around Michelin's test track at racing speed. Colin Snr sees it as another example of Edwards using his brain.

'I always impressed upon Colin from when he was little the importance of the big picture,' says Senior. 'I think that's carried on into the latter part of his racing career. He's a real thinking racer.'

The big picture includes looking at what he's going to do when he quits, Colin has vowed that he will quit bike racing before his 33rd birthday. Hopefully after a couple more world titles. And then what? Car racing? CART? F1? 'I do, I watch it. I'm not an avid watcher,

but when I'm in my motorhome or at home with nothing to do, I'll definitely watch it. Sometimes I'll get up early in the morning to see it in America, but it's not the cornerstone of my weekend. Car racing is also not something I would see myself doing. Two wheels is me, and when two wheels is over I'll be done. What I've learned in life is that life just ain't easy. Everybody thinks us racers are so lucky doing what we do, but a lot of us work so damn hard at it. It's not all peaches and cake. We have to work to do the times to be competitive. Saying that, this is something I have always wanted to do since I was young. If there were a bike to ride, I'd ride it. Now I've got a kid, I'm kinda thinking racing is more of a job. I guess I'm lucky I like doing it, but let me tell ya, I'm looking forward to the day I hang up my helmet for good. Scott Russell didn't start racing until he was 21, but I've been doing this job for about 25 years! When the day comes to quit, I'll just do it. Maybe 31, 32 or 33, whatever. What made Kevin Schwantz such a great champion is that he had the dignity to make the decision when it was right for him. I wanna do it that way too.'

Brands wasn't as good as years gone by. Third and fifth made the title a tough task. (Graeme Brown)

Assen. Tyre woes handed the title to Troy Bayliss. (Graeme Brown)

Turning the Aprilia into a winner would be a tough task. (Gold & Goose)

silly season part two

A factory Honda RC211V on Michelin tyres was what he wanted – and what his fight back to win the 2002 title richly deserved. Instead, halfway through the season, just prior to Edwards reaching his ascendancy in the WSB battle, he was effectively dumped by HRC for 2003.

The ebb and flow of the 2002 season was only to be matched by the machinations of what was to follow. A series of highs and lows, contractual twists and turns, and dead-ends shouldn't happen to someone who had just beaten all the odds against him. But it did, to Honda and HRC's shame.

'Following the fight back for the title, I spent the winter fighting my way through the craziest twists and turns. As it happened, it ended up okay, but at some points I just didn't know where I would wind up. It all

started at the Suzuka 8-Hour back in July. I worked hard for my third win in that prestigious event on the SP-2. That's cool. I was happy and thought Honda would be happy with me. The following Monday morning I had a meeting with Honda executives Koji Nakajima and Silvio Manicardi. I had no idea what shape the meeting was going to take. Then they hit me with it. They started explaining that Honda had lost a bucket-load of money in Europe and were going to cut the budget, and the WSB team might not even exist for 2003. It was kinda like "Look, we may not be here next year so best you can do is start looking around for something else." Looking back, I guess you have to look at the way GPs were going compared with WSB at the time. They build this bike, the Honda VTR1000 SP-2, and only sell so many of them and yet the team

Colin's support system for the past 25 years has included these two important people: wife Alyssia and dad Colin Snr. (Graeme Brown)

costs them many millions of dollars to run. I guess something had to give.'

Indeed. There was a shift in four-stroke racing, with MotoGP going four-stroke in 2002. The pressure was on for WSB to maintain its title as the premier world four-stroke racing formula. It used to be very production based, with bikes being close to the standard road bikes, but over the 15 years of competition, the race machines had developed so much that they were becoming further and further removed from the road bike. So much so that something like Edwards's 2002 SP-2 shares the basic layout of the road bike and little else. In truth, superbikes were becoming less connected to their road-bike brethren. It was no longer a production series and, in many cases, the road-going superbikes didn't even sell as well as other models in manufacturers' line ups. Little wonder that the FireBlade, or its replacement, will be the machine fielded by Honda and HRC in the 2004 WSB championship.

'The Honda guys were pretty much saying that there was nothing for me with them in WSB, as they didn't really think that they would be racing in that class for 2003. I said, "Okay, listen to this. How about we do a new contract for a quarter or half of what I'm making now. I'll take a huge salary cut, but in 2004 I get a GP ride on a V5". I told them I wanted to be Valentino Rossi's team-mate. They said they were

Get off your horse and drink your milk. (Kel Edge)

A home from home. Colin and Alyssia's European home on wheels. (Gold & Goose)

actually looking at Fonsi Nieto to be Rossi's team-mate. From that point on I was like: "You guys are looking at Fonsi Nieto?" It then made sense. It's a sponsor thing again. Politics. I don't kiss enough ass, I guess, and I don't like to get my knees dirty, so what chance do I have? Then soon after the 8-Hour, we heard about the Nicky Hayden deal with HRC. I was pissed off by that! Now, I want to say that this is nothing against Nicky. He's a good guy, a great rider, but I felt that compared with me at my stage of career, with three Suzuka 8-Hour wins and even with just the one WSB title at that time, I was the right person for the ride. I'd been developing the bike and working so hard with Michelin to develop tyres for it. It was a real kick in the guts for me, I can tell you. Maybe they chose Nicky because of the championship position I was in at the time. I was being beaten every other week by Troy. I guess they didn't think I'd win the championship. I guess the only people at that time who thought we still could was me, Adrian and a couple of the guys in my pit.'

At the time, Hayden was on his way to winning the AMA Superbike title for Honda on the SP-2, albeit after an exciting tussle with Eric Bostrom on the venerable old Kawasaki ZX-7R, and his deal wasn't exactly straight forward. The youngster had signed a letter of intent with the factory Yamaha squad in MotoGP. Honda then invoked a clause in his HRC contract, which effectively

stated that if they could beat Yamaha's offer, he'd stay with Honda. They did, he stayed, making negotiations very messy and leaving Yamaha, which was close to telling star rider Max Biaggi he was out of a job, with egg on their faces as they chased a quality rider to link up with Carlos Checa for 2003.

'After all these things going on, I was really pissed at first, but you have to deal with it,' says Edwards. 'Everything that has happened in my career so far has turned out for the better in the end, even if it's not looked that way early on. I'm a believer in the fact that I come from the old school. If you actually ride your ass off, you will eventually get what you deserve.'

But all this left Edwards without a job. It had happened before, but that didn't mean it didn't shake the confidence of the ex-champ at the time.

'Hell, by this time I had a pregnant wife! I was gonna become a dad. I had to have a job,' laughs Colin, 'But seriously, I was a bit anxious about the situation.'

At least he had plenty of time to act and sort himself out with a competitive ride. It was now late July. He was behind Bayliss in the championship, certainly, but he was easily the class of the rest of the field. It wouldn't be too hard to get a ride. And so it proved. Ducati was impressed with the form of the Texan, who was showing all Ducati riders – bar Bayliss – a clean pair of heels in the championship.

Winning two titles means you can spend a little on toys. Colin and Alyssia with their Cadillac. (Kel Edge)

Colin indulging in
one of his big
passions – golf.
(Kel Edge)

Before Gracie
turned up, Colin
and Alyssia had
kids. It's just
that they were
covered with fur.
(Kel Edge)

'Almost as soon as I was back home, the phone rang. It was Ducati. They said they needed help developing the new 999 machine for WSB competition and was I interested? It seemed they were interested thanks to my development with Honda and the SP-1 and SP-2 twins. I was happy that a company like Ducati thought that much of me

All was fine, until Edwards upset the apple cart by going and winning the championship after an epic two-horse struggle.

Fine. The number one plate would rest on the fairing of a 999 for 2003.

'So I've won the championship at Imola. Everything's great. I've done what many thought was impossible and I'm set for next year. Things couldn't have been much better. Then the Monday morning after the win, I'm a little woolly headed, but a guy from Honda rings up – the same guy who back at the 8-Hour said I was out of a job. This time things have changed. He says we will now give me a GP ride, but with Bridgestone tyres. He couldn't say what team I

would be with, he couldn't say a lot of things – there were big holes in what I was being offered. So I was wary and told him straight what I wanted – so much money and (most importantly) a two-year deal with my existing team. I was conscious that if I had to take time out to develop those Bridgestone tyres to work well on the V5 Honda, I had to take my team with me. After all, my Castrol Honda team had done so much to develop tyres with me; it made sense. We'd made close links with Michelin, and that had helped us; we'd just have to do the same with Bridgestone. We could do it. Suddenly the guy comes back to me, guaranteeing everything. The tyres, the team and the money.'

There was just one large, red problem. Ducati. Edwards had signed a letter of intent to ride for Ducati Corse in 2003 and while many riders look at such letters as simply a bargaining tool to secure either a pay hike or another year in an existing contract, Edwards wanted to behave honourably.

'I was thinking, "What do I do now about Ducati?" They'd been so good up until that point, I really didn't

going to run the team, the Honda man I'd been dealing with had passed everything over to him. So Bridgestone sit down with me and say, "Okay, let's negotiate." I'm like, "What? The deal's done." I explained all the previous negotiations I'd gone into up until this point, but the Bridgestone guy told me how it had to be for him – basically starting from zero and haggling all over again. I wasn't too happy. What was the point in carefully getting myself out of the Ducati letter of intent just for this? An agreed deal that wasn't really a deal. The big decisions, when they finally come to be made, aren't really made at the level of Colin Edwards talking to some guy from Honda. They're finally made at a level much higher up than that. And things such as sponsorship have to be taken into account. That's why deals don't always end up as you would expect.'

Understandably upset by the way he'd been treated by Honda, Edwards decided to open the door wide to offers, especially now the promised Honda deal wasn't as cut and dried as he thought it was. A well brought-up young man, Colin believed in behaving in the right way and was stung by the way he'd been treated, especially after he'd delivered the goods for Honda.

'I started thinking about doing things for Colin Edwards, not anyone else,' he says. 'I opened the door to everyone. These people didn't own me; it was up to me to do something about it. Pretty soon I got back in contact with Yamaha and then soon after that Aprilia contacted me. I even had Kawasaki speak to me about the possibility of riding their new ZX-RR.'

Returning to the Yamaha fold did look like a possibility. 'As I mentioned,' says Edwards, 'it's a corporate thing and even though it did look likely at one stage that I would ride a four-stroke M1 alongside Checa or in the satellite team, I just wasn't part of the top-level boardroom plan. It was as simple as that.'

But it wasn't without effort from both sides. Edwards spoke to many old friends at Yamaha America and Europe during the final negotiations, and to triple 500cc world champ Wayne Rainey. Rainey, who had won his titles with Yamaha and been team manager for the marque, still had connections.

'I thought we were making progress with Yamaha,' explains Colin, 'and I think some of the Yamaha guys I

want to cause them any trouble, but I also wanted to be in GPs with my old Castrol Honda team. It was just too good an opportunity to pass up. I needn't have worried. The people at Ducati were just great about the whole thing. I went to Ducati and asked about how we could work out things. They were simply awesome about the whole thing. They knew my desires to go GP racing and despite having a letter of intent, they said they didn't want to hold me back. Top people. It must have left them a little pissed, as I had signed something, but what can I say. They were excellent.'

What a turnaround. Three days after the Imola race and Edwards is finally going into GPs with his existing team on the dominant Honda RC211V V5 four-stroke GP missile (a machine which had won all but two of the MotoGP races that year). And they had a two-year deal to help develop the new Bridgestone tyres.

Things didn't stay that simple for long.

'A little while goes by and pretty soon I get a call from a guy at Bridgestone. It seems that as they are

was talking to thought so too, but, in the end, it wasn't their or my decision to make.'

Suddenly, another offer came in from Aprilia.

The 2002 season had seen the remarkable Aprilia RS3 'Cube' debut in the MotoGP championship. It was an in-line triple, built by Cosworth Racing, which manufactures engines for Formula 1, Indy Car racing and the World Rally Car championship. It was, effectively, a slither of an F1 engine, featuring pneumatic valves, a fly-by-wire throttle and mucho power – around 220bhp at 14,500rpm. Regis Laconi had won the chance to debut the bike in the 2002 GP series by winning one of the last WSB races in 2001 for Aprilia, at Imola. But you would almost think he rued the day. Ask him what it was like to ride and he'd mimic hanging on for dear life. The RS3 is not for the shy and retiring…

'No matter what the bike did in 2002,' says Edwards, 'Aprilia is a technologically advanced team. They've won so much. They don't simply want to make up the numbers in MotoGP. With this in mind they had me interested.'

To make it all work, Edwards wanted the tyres and the team to do it. 'I was real insistent on the Michelin tyres – Aprilia had worked with Dunlop during the 2002 season with the RS3. I pushed and pushed all the Michelin guys I knew and so did Aprilia, as they knew how important it was to me, so when eventually Michelin said yes, they'd supply the tyres, the Aprilia deal looked very attractive. They were trying to accommodate me and that was appreciated.'

Then it happened again. With the deal looking set – but at least with no ink on it, this time – Castrol contacted Colin and wanted to talk. They didn't want to lose him after five years together. It seemed that his Castrol Honda team-boss Neil Tuxworth had been beavering away behind the scenes trying to put the Bridgestone deal together.

'They made me an offer to ride on the Honda V5, with my old team but again on Bridgestone tyres. It was interesting and it was flattering. So now I had two options, Honda with Bridgestones or Aprilia with Michelin. I didn't have what I thought to be a 'ride and win' deal; maybe only Nicky Hayden, Valentino Rossi and a couple of others had that – a Honda V5 on Michelins.

So I had to make a decision but I needed help from someone who could understand what I was going through. So I spoke to Wayne Rainey again and explained the situation. Wayne did help,' smiles Edwards. 'Kinda! He told me it was just my decision to make when it came to my future and I had to make it on my own. He explained that neither ride was exactly what I wanted, so I had to decide what would make me feel better. He didn't want to make the decision for me. He just made a few things clear. He's a real professional, is Wayne.'

Things came to a head in the Edwards's household on the morning of the Phillip Island MotoGP race, a location 17 hours ahead of Edwards's home in Montgomery, Texas. The first call came early in the morning from Nicholas Goubert, the head man for Michelin's motorcycle racing arm, confirming that the French company would supply tyres to the Aprilia team if Edwards was going to join. A few hours later, Tuxworth called to say that the deal for Colin to ride a V5 in Castrol colours, with his old team, but on

Anything he
puts his hand
to, be it tennis...
(Gold & Goose)

...or rock climbing.
He'll give it his all.
(Jim Press)

Bridgestone tyres. At last, a decision could be made.

'Eventually I realised that I didn't want to make my MotoGP debut on tyres that I didn't know at all. The Michelins on the other hand… well, I couldn't and didn't want to turn my back on them as they'd been so good to me for so long. We'd been working together for so long to get the tyres right, it seemed that the right thing to do was to stay.'

So, Edwards plumped for the Aprilia deal and told them that he was going to sign for them. Then another deal came around, this time from the Sito Pons-run satellite Honda squad.

'He'd been talking to me on-and-off,' says Colin, 'but not making any firm offers. Suddenly it's all on again. Almost a dream ride: his team, Castrol backing, Michelin tyres and the Honda RC211V, the most competitive package out there. So by now I'm thinking, "Oh no, not again. I've now got to try and tell Aprilia what's happening. I was helped by the fact that it wasn't that straightforward. Pons wanted

money from Castrol, a lot of money from Castrol, say around $5m, to secure the deal – maybe twice as much as Castrol wanted to put in. Rumour has it the RC211Vs cost twice as much to lease as a stroker NSR. In the end, Castrol wanted to be involved and we'd built up a great relationship over the years, but it was too big a financial step. I guess they wanted to make a much smaller step into GPs and I respect that. So another boardroom decision comes out negative. There was another aborted attempt, putting together Pons, Bridgestone and Castrol, but that was no different to the other offer.'

The single bewildering fact remained that Honda and HRC wanted a comparatively internationally unproven (though undoubtedly talented) youngster on the best bike in the MotoGP paddock, rather than a proven winner. Edwards's rival Troy Bayliss summed up the whole bizarre situation when he said of Honda's shameful negotiations: 'What's wrong with those guys? Are they stupid?'

With the decision made, Edwards still had to wait a little while before he could fly out, see the factory for himself and sign on the dotted line.

At last, it would be Edwards, Aprilia and Michelin for 2003.

'What eventually turned me around to the Aprilia deal? I guess they wanted me and they wanted to accommodate me. They believed that with the right people around me, they knew, that I knew I could make it work.'

Edwards finally flew to Italy to secure the deal. He met Ivan Beggio, head of Aprilia, and saw the factory set-up for himself.

'Me and Ivan had a long chat the day I inked the deal. What impressed me was the fact that he's really just a race fan, who wants to go win. I liked that, it's just like me.'

Everything looked good, but what of his team? Aprilia had a professional set-up to go with the RS3 into GPs, but the main battle in developing a bike is communication. Colin knew that he had to get some elements of his old team to come with him. But with 'his' Castrol Honda team moving into the British Superbike championship for 2003 with Steve Plater on Edwards's 2002 VTRs, in preperation for a 2004 return to WSB, he had to act fast.

'I knew who I wanted,' says Edwards. 'I wanted Adrian Gorst to come with me into GPs. He had things set up with Castrol Honda in British Superbikes. He lives in the UK so it would have been easy for him to stay, but I didn't want to let go. I pestered him and even put his email address on my website so the fans would bombard him with emails telling him to stay. Eventually, we managed to make him an offer that he couldn't refuse.'

Gorst – the typically dependable, relentless, methodical Kiwi – would join Edwards, even if it was without the lucky ten-gallon hat that had seen them through the 2002 season.

And that wasn't all. Edwards wasn't done yet. His main contact at Michelin from his Castrol Honda days, John Bolton, came with him as well as Gorst's Castrol Honda teamster Craig Burton. This gives Edwards the same nucleus of the team that believed in him when he set about Bayliss's 58-point lead in the 2002 WSB series.

'That's the genius of this deal,' says Edwards, 'getting guys like Adrian, John and Craig around me. We will gel with the Aprilia guys, no question, but we need to have some continuity with what's gone before. We work well together.'

By the time the final deal was (at last) sorted with Aprilia, Colin had time to reflect on what had happened. The winter had, effectively, mirrored the season's twists and turns and been almost as dramatic, making it a hell of an end to a hell of a year.

'A few times during all these negotiations, I was kinda thinking, "Man, we're not trying to broker world peace or nothin', we're just trying to sort out things so a bunch of guys can go around and ride in circles and stuff".'

By the time the UK's annual motorcycle show at the National Exhibition Centre came around in November he still had press and public engagements to honour for Honda. On press day at the NEC show, Colin stood on the Honda stand where it had just been announced that his old WSB team and bikes would be taking part in the

British Superbike series for 2003. Castrol Honda team boss Neil Tuxworth fielded questions about why the move had been made, but just as proceedings were drawing to a close, Colin interrupted.

'I just wanna say that I'd like to thank Neil for taking a chance on a punk kid from Texas. Thanks a lot to the team as well.'

It was as poignant a moment as you can get in the cut-and-thrust, merciless world of bike racing. One thing was certain, there was a lot of mutual respect between Tuxworth and Edwards.

'When he joined our team back in 1998 he wasn't at the level he is now,' says Tuxworth. 'He worked at it. Look at the results in WSB. Fifth in our first year together, second in 1999, first in 2000, second and then first again in 2002. Few have worked harder.'

But Edwards's future was with Aprilia and MotoGP. 'I always wanted to go into GPs. I didn't want to get to, say, 32 or so, be about to quit and yet not have tried GPs. When I signed for Ducati, it was known that Troy would be heading to GPs after the 2002 WSB

year, so I was lined up to be alongside Neil Hodgson. At the time I thought, "Perhaps that's it. Perhaps I'm destined to stay in superbikes forever. I guess it's what I was meant to do." Up until then I'd always figured that I'd either not had the right passport to get into GPs, not had enough sponsorship to take to a team, or a combination of both, but by now I was just pleased that all the shenanigans of the previous few months were over.'

Interestingly, his team-mate on the Aprilia RS3 Cube was going to be Noriyuki Haga. For the past few years the two had seen their careers overlap. The pair took victory in the 1996 Suzuka 8-Hour race. Haga had taken the old YZF to a victory in WSB after Edwards had spent years trying, and Colin had beaten Haga to the 2000 WSB title following the drug debacle. Haga, who had shone on the four-cylinder Yamahas, moved to GPs with the Red Bull Yamaha squad but subsequently failed to shine on the two-stroke, before moving back to WSB on the Aprilia RSV Mille. It would be interesting to watch the pair work together and it

If he tries half as hard at fatherhood as he does at his sport, Gracie is one very luck lady... (Gold & Goose)

After all the worry, an Aprilia man at last. (Gold & Goose)

would be even more interesting to see these two, with such contrasting styles, ride the Aprilia RS3 Cube.

The Cube may be a beautiful bit of kit, but effectively it's a three-cylinder hammer to crack a walnut. And a pneumatically driven hammer at that. Why? Well, because the Aprilia is alone in the MotoGP paddock in relying on pneumatically operated valves, a method of closing them quicker and more effectively than standard cams and springs. Cosworth Racing in the UK developed the engine. These are the same people who build engines for the Indy Car series in the US and the motors used in the Jaguar Formula One programme. Understandably, they've stuck with what they know in the design of the Cube motor and pneumatic valves and fly-by-wire throttles is what they know best. The company has worked with Aprilia before, having a hand in the original road and race RSV-R Mille engines. So with their background it comes as no real surprise to find out that this motor is, in effect, Formula One's bastard son. Pneumatic valves shut each of the four valves in each of the three cylinders. The deal with using pneumatically closed valves rather than traditional steel springs is that springs are

only really effective to around 16-17,000rpm; pneumatically closed valves are good to a ceiling of around 20-22,000 revs, which eventually means more power. Power wasn't an issue, even in the Cube's debut year, because it was rumoured to be pumping out 220bhp-plus, with a good spread of power from 9,000rpm up to peak power output at 14,500rpm.

This Cube was the first of the four-strokes to crack the 200mph barrier at Mugello in 2002, hitting 200.7mph in the Saturday afternoon qualifying session for Sunday's race. The fly-by-wire throttle dispenses with the traditional cable and uses ECUs to do part of the work. In more traditional applications, fly-by-wire uses computers to do the work of the hydraulics or cables. But FIM regulations (where the throttle must close in the event of a crash) means that a cable actually operates the butterfly valve in the required direction. It's only when you twist the throttle that you're opening the butterflies through the ECU and the computer. Again, this method should confer some advantages as the drive-by-wire system means you can program the throttle response more precisely than the rider can and it also gives more options for the future

The winter saw slow, steady progress on the Cube. (Getty Images)

Preparing to go out in his first qualifying session in MotoGP at Suzuka. (Gold & Goose)

with things like launch control. Sounds like a racer's dream, doesn't it? But it would be fair to say the Cube suffered from a lack of development in 2002 resulting from a lack of funds. The best results in the bike's debut season were two eighth places at the opening round at Suzuka in Japan and a fifth at Mugello, Italy.

A lack of cash meant the bike was over the minimum weight by a fair margin in its first year of racing. It was also, with the Suzuki GSV-R, one of the last bikes to be readied for the new four-stroke MotoGP season.

In 2002, money was diverted to the 250cc campaign – which Aprilia desperately wanted to win – and the WSB team. Marco Melandri won the title in 2002 and for 2003 the WSB team and the 60° V-twin Mille is no more. With Haga joining Edwards in the GP set-up, the cash is now freed up for the bike's diet and development in the 2003 season. The diet has been a strict one. In 2002 the bike was way over the 135kg limit for three-cylinder machines. During early testing in 2003, despite the use of lighter, more expensive (and more exotic) materials the bike was still tipping the scales 10kg over the limit, or bang on the limit for four and five cylinder machines.

One thing to consider is the fact that the Cube certainly seems to have the most potential in the paddock. Even some of Honda's engineering staff were keeping a watchful eye on the Aprilia pit when it made its debut at Suzuka in 2002.

So Edwards was heading to GPs with a machine with loads of untapped potential. This meant lots of hard work.

'We needed to go testing straight away as I knew we'd have some work to do on the bike.'

His first taste of the machine he'd be riding for 2003 came at Jerez, Spain, in November 2002. The track is a stalwart of the GP testing scene, and one which Colin, with his WSB background, had never even seen before. He was on only his fourth lap, it was damp and he was exiting Curva Sito Pons, hitting fourth gear, cramming himself behind the bubble to slingshot himself down the back-straight. He felt the rear begin to slide. He shut the throttle, but the bike continued to slide until the throttle finally shut off. The rear tyre then gripped and the seat pad kicked him into orbit. 'I told her to back down, but she didn't, so she told me to fuck off! I shut the throttle when I thought it would be best and there was a fraction of a second's delay and the rear kept spinning and I went for a slide.'

Welcome to MotoGP, Colin. The Aprilia, after his user-friendly Honda, must have felt like a cruel mistress.

The astonishing fact is that up until then, his laser reactions had ensured no high-sides since early 1996. A high-side, with the exception of hitting other bikes or trackside furniture, is the most feared of all bike racing crashes. When a rear-wheel slide starts to become uncontrollable, the natural reaction is to back off the throttle. The rear tyre, which could be inches to a foot out of line and spinning wildly, suddenly finds grip as the power is shut off and pulls the bike into line suddenly. The resultant snap comes with the force of a whipcrack, punting the rider's posterior and other body parts into the kind of trajectory that only astronauts are used to. Edwards reckons that it was going to happen. 'First lap, fourth lap, last lap, whatever. It's a feeling thing that you have to get used to. I had never ridden with a fly-by-wire throttle before so it was all-new to me. I knew me and the Aprilia had to learn each other fast.'

What a wake-up call. Just over 11 minutes into his GP test debut and he was on his back sliding towards the gravel. It was his first crash in 2002 since July at the Laguna round of the WSB championship. The crash left him with a gash in his left elbow that required stitches. It also told him all he wanted to know about the Aprilia, even compared with the Honda RCV, which he'd ridden in one of its earlier forms. 'Compared with the RCV I rode at Suzuka just after the 8-Hour, the Aprilia makes the Honda seem real docile and almost made my title winning SP-2 feel like a woman's bike! I was a bit surprised as I'd heard a lot of stuff about the Aprilia but to me it felt phenomenal, as if it had a lot of potential. I expected it to be a big wake up call and that's just what it was.'

The crash ruled him out of the rest of that day's testing, but he got back on the RS3 for the second day, testing different Michelin wet, intermediate and slick tyres.

Another test at Jerez followed, before moving to Valencia, a track Colin knows well. For crew chief Gorst, this was effectively where the work would begin. 'We'd only been to Jerez before, which is somewhere me and Colin hadn't been to previously, so we'd not really been to any racetracks where we had any baseline settings. It would be different at Valencia, as we knew the track and figured that we'd be able to make some headway.'

The RS3 was still a handful, especially around the tight turns of Circuito Ricardo Tormo. 'Dude, see the motif of the bull I'm riding on the back of my leathers?' Colin would say pointing over his shoulders. 'That's just what it's like riding the RS3.' Cue toothy grin.

Valencia proved to be a turning point. On day one Edwards managed to equal his best ever time around the Spanish track – a 1m 34.8s lap. On the VTR, it was done with the aid of qualifying rubber, but on the RS3 it was done with race tyres. He shaved a further three tenths off on day two of the test, but still wasn't 100 per cent happy, as he knew that he'd have to go a fair bit quicker (like by a second) to get close to a consistent race pace. During this first Valencia test, Edwards and crew chief Gorst were troubled a little by the front-end patter that was dictating corner speed.

'We have all the top-end power you could wish for with the Cube, but it's about getting it down to the ground. At that Valencia test, the power and speed was giving us the lap time, but I didn't want to rely on the motor.'

After riding a twin, it didn't come as much of a surprise to find that Edwards was working with Gorst and the Aprilia technicians to try to smooth out the Aprilia's engine mapping and take the peaky edge off the power delivery.

'We spent a lot of time working on various ECU software, with various ignition mappings to try and smooth things out. The bike was quite peaky, maybe a bit too peaky for me.'

By the time of the second Valencia test in January, changes had made the bike much more to Colin's liking. He ended up equalling the 2002 pole position time of Max Biaggi's Yamaha M1, setting a 1m 33.2s lap.

'Everyone wanted to know what we did with the bike, but if we told people everyone would do it! It transformed the bike, so that it became a real pleasure to ride. We also received some new parts that changed a few things. I ended up counting the days before I got to ride the thing again. We found the half-a-second that would have seen us dice for the lead in 2002, but we all knew that we'd need to find the other half-second, or more, that everyone finds somehow during the winter. It's just been like a puzzle. You have to find the right combination of what works and what doesn't. Aprilia and Adrian are good at that.'

Rumour had it that there were some major changes to the frame and chassis to make it more to his liking.

People were beginning to sit up and take notice. A string of tests against other MotoGP regulars saw Edwards hovering near the top of the pile in the competitive back-to-back tests.

Even ex-boss Tuxworth was impressed. 'He was doing better for Aprilia than even I thought he would. There's nothing wrong with Colin Edwards. It's what he's up against and who he's up against. That's why I still think the best he can hope for is top six. The bikes he's up against are the Hondas; they're

By the start of 2003, Colin and the RS3 were appearing in the official colours of the Alice Aprilia Team (Gold & Goose)

so dominant. This is nothing against Aprilia as they've done well, but the simple fact is they don't have the resources of Honda. Colin has the experience and he can do well, but even if Valentino Rossi was on that Aprilia he wouldn't beat the Honda. I truly believe on a Honda Colin could beat anyone else out there.'

So why wasn't he given a Honda to take on the world in MotoGP in 2004? 'It was sad for Colin and Honda that he never got the chance to ride in MotoGP for the company,' admits Neil. 'He did a tremendous amount for Honda but for various political reasons it wasn't to be. It's always going to be a sad loss for both Honda and Colin.'

Another ex-team boss feels Edwards has the tools to succeed in MotoGP. 'I think he moved to MotoGP at the right time,' says Davide Brivio of the Yamaha GP team, 'because he is now mature and the bikes are four-strokes, which he has great experience of. It depends on the level of his bike but I expect him to go on the podium some times.'

On the way back from the Valencia test Edwards had to rush to hospital as Alyssia had been experiencing contractions. As it is for many soon-to-be parents, it turned out to be a false alarm. Both were sent home, but warned that the time was at hand. Colin was desperate to be at the birth, which sat uneasily close to a 'window' where he was planning to be at home during what was a busy test schedule.

'If I was in Europe and I got "the call" I'd be on the first plane out of there.'

As it happened he needn't have worried. On the afternoon of 21 January, the labour induction process began and at 2am the following morning they were the proud parents of a baby girl, Gracie Kayte Edwards, a 7lb 5oz bundle of joy that made the Edwards family complete.

Two world titles, three Suzuka 8-Hour wins, national titles, race wins, they all immediately fell into perspective with the more important job of fatherhood.

'People always said it was a life-changing thing,' said Colin after the event. 'I wasn't looking forward to that as I liked my life the way it was. But what people didn't say was that being a parent changes things for the better.'

career
highlights

(Gold & Goose)

1991

First full year of racing as an amateur on a 600 Honda, a Honda RC30 and Yamaha TZ250. He won every race he finished and was unbeaten in his amateur career winning a record five national titles in the AMA/CCS Race of Champions at Daytona and a record eight national titles in the WERA/GNF meeting at Road Atlanta.

First Pro 250cc GP November 1991, 2nd

1992

250cc GP highlights
AMA 250cc GP champion, with five wins at Daytona Beach, Charlotte, Brainerd, Lexington and College Station.

(Gold & Goose)

AMA Superbike highlights 1993–94

1993

Round	Event	Date	Position
1	Phoenix International Raceway	15 February	4th
2	Daytona International Speedway	7 March	DNF
3	Laguna Seca	18 April	4th
4	Charlotte Motor Speedway	1 May	2nd
5	Road America, Elkhart Lake	13 June	DNF
6	New Hampshire International Speedway	20 June	DNF
7	Road Atlanta	18 July	DNF
8	Brainerd International Raceway	1 August	4th
9	Mid-Ohio Sports Car Course	8 August	6th
10	Sears Point	28 August	7th

FINAL STANDINGS – 1 Doug Polen 326; 2 Dale Quarterly 263; 3 Miguel DuHamel 261; 4 Jamie James 230; 5 Takahiro Sohwa; 6 Edwards 189

(Gold & Goose)

(Gold & Goose)

1994

1	Daytona International Speedway	13 March	DNF
2	Phoenix International Raceway	27 March	3rd
3	Pomona Fairplex	10 April	DNF
4	Laguna Seca	22 May	DNF
5	Road America, Elkhart Lake	12 June	DNF
6	Loudon, New Hampshire	19 June	5th
7	Mid-Ohio Sports Car Course	7 July	1st
8	Brainerd International Raceway	31 July	1st
9	Sears Point Raceway	21 August	1st
10	Road Atlanta	18 September	3rd

FINAL STANDINGS – 1 Troy Corser 273; 2 Jamie James 272; 3 Takahiro Sohwa 251; 4 Pascal Picotte 245; 5 Edwards 239

World Superbike highlights 1995-2002

(Gold & Goose)

1995

Round	Event	Date	Race 1/Race 2
1	Germany, Hockenheim	7 May	7th/5th
2	Italy, Misano	21 May	Out of points/DNF
3	Great Britain, Donington Park	28 May	Out of points/12th
4	San Marino, Monza	18 June	3rd/5th
5	Spain, Albacete	25 June	10th/11th
6	Austria, Salzburgring	9 July	9th/DNF
7	US, Laguna Seca	23 July	8th/9th
8	Europe, Brands Hatch	6 August	5th/2nd
9	Japan, Sugo	27 August	6th/10th
10	Holland, Assen	10 September	DNF/6th
11 & 12	Indonesia and Australia, Phillip Island, missed due to death of Yasutomo Nagai		

FINAL STANDINGS – 1 Fogarty 478; 2 Corser 339; 3 Slight 323; 4 Gobert 222; 5 Nagai 188; 11 Edwards 144

(Gold & Goose)

1996

1	San Marino, Misano	14 April	11th/7th
2	Great Britain, Donington Park	28 April	6th/4th
3	Germany, Hockenheim	12 May	3rd/5th
4	Italy, Monza	16 June	3rd/5th
5	Czech Republic, Brno	30 June	6th/7th
6	US, Laguna Seca	21 July	4th/DNF
7	Europe, Brands Hatch	4 August	4th/3rd
8	Indonesia, Sentul	18 August	5th/4th
9	Japan, Sugo	25 August	DNS/DNS
10	Holland, Assen	8 September	DNS/DNS
11	Spain, Albacete	6 October	2nd/3rd
12	Australia, Phillip Island	27 October	2nd/3rd

FINAL STANDINGS – 1 Corser 369; 2 Slight 347; 3 Kocinski 337; 4 Fogarty 331; 5 Edwards 248

(Gold & Goose)

1997

1	Australia, Phillip Island	23 March	DNF/2nd
2	San Marino, Misano	20 April	6th/8th
3	Great Britain, Donington Park	4 May	5th/6th
4	Germany, Hockenheim	8 June	7th/5th

FINAL STANDINGS – 1 Kocinski 416; 2 Fogarty 358; 3 Slight 343;
4 Yanagawa 247; 5 Crafar 234; 12 Edwards 79

1998

1	Australia, Phillip Island	22 March	7th/7th
2	Great Britain, Donington Park	13 April	6th/7th
3	Italy, Monza	10 May	1st/1st
4	Spain, Albacete	24 May	5th/DNF
5	Germany, Nürburgring	7 June	2nd/2nd
6	San Marino, Misano	21 June	3rd/4th
7	South Africa, Kyalami	5 July	9th/4th
8	US, Laguna Seca	12 July	11th/10th
9	Europe, Brands Hatch	2 August	1st/4th
10	Austria, A1-Ring	30 August	7th/9th
11	Holland, Assen	6 September	5th/5th
12	Japan, Sugo	4 October	13th/13th

FINAL STANDINGS – 1 Fogarty 351.5; 2 Slight 347; 3 Corser 328.5;
4 Chili 293.5; 5 Edwards 279.5

(Gold & Goose)

1999

1	South Africa, Kyalami	28 March	5th/4th
2	Australia, Phillip Island	18 April	3rd/3rd
3	Great Britain, Donington Park	2 May	3rd/1st
4	Spain, Albacete	16 May	DNF/1st
5	Italy, Monza	30 May	2nd/2nd
6	Germany, Nürburgring	13 June	DNF/4th
7	San Marino, Misano	27 June	6th/7th
8	US, Laguna Seca	11 July	4th/5th
9	Europe, Brands Hatch	1 August	1st/1st
10	Austria, A1-Ring	29 August	1st/8th
11	Holland, Assen	5 September	5th/5th
12	Germany, Hockenheim	12 September	4th/5th
13	Japan, Sugo	10 October	9th/9th

FINAL STANDINGS – 1 Fogarty 489; 2 Edwards 361; 3 Corser 361;
4 Slight 323; 5 Yanagawa 308; 6 Chili 251.
Edwards takes second with win countback

(Gold & Goose)

2000

1	South Africa, Kyalami	2 April	1st/1st
2	Australia, Phillip Island	23 April	5th/5th
3	Japan, Sugo	30 April	5th/3rd

(Gold & Goose)

4	Great Britain, Donington Park	14 May	1st/DNF
5	Italy, Monza	21 May	2nd/1st
6	Germany, Hockenheim	4 June	4th/2nd
7	San Marino, Misano	18 June	DNF/10th
8	Spain, Valencia	25 June	5th/4th
9	US, Laguna Seca	9 July	2nd/4th
10	Europe 1, Brands Hatch	6 August	10th/6th
11	Holland, Assen	3 September	1st/5th
12	Germany, Oschersleben	10 September	1st/1st
13	Europe 2, Brands Hatch	15 October	8th/1st

FINAL STANDINGS – 1 Edwards 400; 2 Haga 335; 3 Corser 310;
4 Chili 258; 5 Yanagawa 247

2001

1	Spain, Valencia	11 March	6th/4th
2	South Africa, Kyalami	1 Aprill	1st/DNF
3	Australia, Phillip Island	22 April	1st/Cancelled due to bad weather
4	Japan, Sugo	29 April	12th/13th
5	Italy, Monza	13 May	2nd/2nd
6	Great Britain, Donington Park	27 May	5th/6th
7	Germany, Lausitzring	10 June	1st/3rd
8	San Marino, Misano	24 June	3rd/11th
9	US, Laguna Seca	8 July	6th/6th
10	Europe, Brands Hatch	29 July	3rd/5th
11	Germany, Oschersleben	2 September	1st/2nd
12	Holland, Assen	9 September	3rd/10th
13	Imola, Autodromo Enzo & Dino Ferrari	30 September	3rd/DNF

FINAL STANDINGS – 1 Bayliss 369; 2 Edwards 333; 3 Bostrom 312;
4 Corser 284; 5 Hodgson 269

(Gold & Goose)

2002

1	Spain, Valencia	10 March	4th/3rd
2	Australia, Phillip Island	24 March	2nd/2nd
3	South Africa, Kyalami	7 April	2nd/3rd
4	Japan, Sugo	21 April	1st/2nd
5	Italy, Monza	12 May	3rd/2nd
6	Great Britain, Silverstone	26 May	1st/2nd
7	Germany, Lausitzring	9 June	2nd/2nd
8	San Marino, Misano	23 June	2nd/2nd
9	US, Laguna Seca	14 July	3rd/1st
10	Europe, Brands Hatch	28 July	1st/1st
11	Germany, Oschersleben	1 September	1st/1st
12	Holland, Assen	8 September	1st/1st
13	Imola, Autodromo Enzo & Dino Ferrari	29 September	1st/1st

FINAL STANDINGS – 1 Edwards 552; 2 Bayliss 541; 3 Hodgson 326;
4 Haga 278; 5 B Bostrom

(Gold & Goose)

index